WHAT I WISH SOMEONE HAD TOLD ME
ABOUT THE FIRST FIVE YEARS OF MARRIAGE

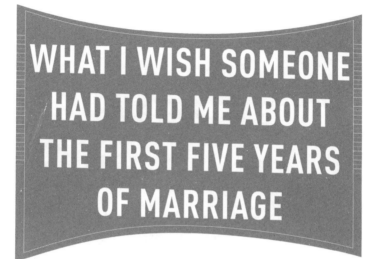

WHAT I WISH SOMEONE HAD TOLD ME ABOUT THE FIRST FIVE YEARS OF MARRIAGE

Roy Petitfils

ST. ANTHONY MESSENGER PRESS
Cincinnati, Ohio

"Breathing Under Water" is used by permission of its author, Sister Carol Bielecki, R.S.J.C.

Scripture passages have been taken from the *New Revised Standard Version Bible,* copyright ©1989 by the Division of Christian Education of the National Council of the Churches of Christ in the U.S.A., and used by permission. All rights reserved.

Cover and book design by Mark Sullivan
Cover image: © www.gettyimages.com/Stockbyte

LIBRARY OF CONGRESS CATALOGING-IN-PUBLICATION DATA
Petitfils, Roy.
What I wish someone had told me about the first five years of marriage / Roy Petitfils.
     p. cm.
Includes bibliographical references.
ISBN 978-0-86716-853-2 (pbk. : alk. paper) 1. Marriage—Religious aspects—Christianity. I. Title.
BV835.P49 2010
248.8'44—dc22
                    2009043160

ISBN 978-0-86716-853-2

Published by St. Anthony Messenger Press
28 W. Liberty St.
Cincinnati, OH 45202
www.SAMPBooks.org

Printed in the United States of America.

Printed on acid-free paper.

10 11 12 13 14   5 4 3 2 1

For my wife, Mindi, who loves me into becoming
a better person each day. I love you.
Thank you for loving me.

· CONTENTS

I must first thank Lyn Doucet, who made this book possible. Thank you for introducing me to Lisa Biedenbach whose vision for this project was the original inspiration. Thank you, Lisa, for taking the time to meet with me and for giving me an opportunity to be a part of this project and the St. Anthony Messenger Press family. Thank you for truly caring about your authors—in sickness and in health.

A special thanks to my editor, Mary Curran-Hackett, who worked with this young author, and in the process made the manuscript more practical and readable. You challenged me to look through a wider lens and helped me to become a better writer and thinker.

To my friend Christopher Meaux, a good writer himself, who first believed in my ability to write. To my friend and mentor Mike Patin who encouraged me to write with the words, "If you want to write, then write!"

To Susan Charbonnet, Barbara Melebeck, and Diane Kincel— your support and encouragement made this manuscript possible. Thanks for your unwavering commitment to your ministry, Crossroads Catholic Bookstore.

To Matthew Hebert who offered clear theological insight and Dan Jurek, my friend and mentor, whose personal commitment to the sacrament of marriage shines powerfully in his own family and the many he helps to support through his counseling at Pax Renewal Center.

To the many couples who shared their journeys with me, some of whom allowed me to share their stories here, I am truly grateful.

I am especially grateful to the communities of Sacred Heart Church and St. Cecilia School who loved and supported me through what has been a long and sometimes arduous journey. In particular the support of Father Louis Richard, my pastor, and George Fontenot, my principal, who allowed me the flexibility needed to complete this manuscript.

Mostly, I am grateful for the love, support, and affirmation of my bride, Mindi. In our sacrament you patiently walk with me as we seek to live out God's plan for our marriage. Thank you for allowing me to see God in you and for consistently reminding me of the same God who dwells in me. I look forward to spending the rest of our lives together with our two precious sons, Max and Benjamin.

"The desire and ability of a man and woman to form a lasting bond of love and life in marriage are written into their nature."

—from *Married Love and the Gift of Life*,
The Committee of Pro-Life Activities of the
United States Conference of Catholic Bishops

"God comes to us disguised as our life."

—Paula D'Arcy

From the Wedding to Married Life

Each day in our country nearly six thousand couples get married, totaling 2.2 million weddings per year. With the cost of a wedding averaging $20,000, it should come as no surprise that the U.S. wedding industry represents a multibillion-dollar market. Driving this booming industry are couples who focus enormous amounts of energy on planning the perfect ceremony and leave themselves little time to explore the complexities of building a strong and enduring marriage.

In one episode of the sitcom *Everybody Loves Raymond,* Ray (Ray Romano) and his wife Debra (Patricia Heaton) are having a flashback of when they were planning their wedding day. Ray says to Debra: "You're already planning the wedding?" and Debra responds by saying that she's been planning the wedding since she was twelve. Ray seems incredulous, because he realizes she hadn't even met him until she was twenty-two. Without missing a beat Debra zings, "Well, you're the last piece of the puzzle."

This humorous example illustrates the all too common reality of how one can easily become preoccupied with the wedding ceremony. There is nothing wrong with wanting and planning a beautiful wedding. However, a couple should be just as committed to planning a beautiful *marriage.* That's where this book comes in.

If you are reading this book, perhaps it is because you sense something of the importance and sacredness in marriage. You want to give your marriage the very best chance to "make it." Somewhere inside you feel a desire to have a great relationship, one marked by deep intimacy, joy, and significance.

I share those same desires. I am convinced that it is not only possible for marriages to thrive, but that it is God's plan for marriage. God designed marriage to be joyful. I once believed the words of a newlywed friend, that, "things will just work themselves out." After seven years of marriage and working with couples as a therapist, I've learned that relationships succeed because *we* work things out. Marriages are not self-sustaining and do not survive on autopilot. They require constant attention and intentional effort.

But it can be rewarding effort. It can be an adventure! And like any adventure it is not easy. There are unexpected detours, obstacles, and challenges. But there are also thrills, excitement, and happiness. God designed marriage this way. God desires for us to experience this fullness of grace and life.

What's the Big Deal About the First Five Years?

Once the plane touches the tarmac and the honeymoon is over, the sobering reality of making a relationship work sets in. During the first five years of marriage, individual goals, desires, and values that were not clarified before the wedding are illuminated and sometimes come into sharp contrast with those of our spouse. This is the time period when a couple makes major decisions about such things as lifestyle, career, having and raising children, and financial planning, to name but a few.

Between 40 and 50 percent of all marriages will end in divorce. A marriage is most at risk for divorce in its first five years. Some marriage therapists suggest that how a couple navigates their first five years is a good indicator of whether or not their marriage will succeed.

Why Marriage Anyway?

In the movie *Four Christmases*, Brad (Vince Vaughn) and Kate (Reese Witherspoon), a happily unmarried cohabitating couple, flee their families every year at Christmas, under the guise of doing mission work in other countries. When their flight to Fiji is cancelled and they are caught by a news reporter on camera at the airport, they are forced to visit their families for Christmas—all four of them.

What ensues is a day long odyssey, visiting each of their divorced parents. At the end of the day Brad is relieved to not be in the same predicament as his parents, while Kate feels that their life together, while fun and thrilling, lacks the significance she sees in her mom's and sister's who are wives and mothers.

Kate and Brad represent a growing number of couples who are choosing to delay marriage. Between the years 1960 and 2006 the number of couples not married increased more than twelvefold. Studies indicate that more than half of couples who marry for the first time lived together before their wedding. Some see cohabitation as its own acceptable alternative to marriage or living alone. And yet for many other couples, for varying reasons, cohabitation is a precursor to tying the knot.

When I asked a couple who were friends of mine why they cohabitated before they got married, they in essence said, "If things didn't work out, well, at least we found out before we made it permanent by getting married." This couple, like a growing number of young couples today, had witnessed firsthand the dark side of a marriage gone bad. They were some of the growing number of children who lived through a divorce and are committed to making sure that doesn't happen to them or their children. I believe that for many couples who cohabitate, their desire to live together before marriage is not taking the easy road, but in their minds, taking the *safe* road.

There are other reasons people choose cohabitation. Some find that it just makes good economic sense to live together. In lieu of paying two separate rents or mortgages and the work of maintaining two separate residences, some choose the seemingly more practical alternative of living together. For others who are already having sex before marriage, living together is often seen as a logical "next step" in their relationship.

Some envision married life as an infringement on their freedom. The prospect of saying no to single life, the dating scene, and even one's privacy can be scary. Marriage helped me to discover a new meaning of freedom. I learned from the psychiatrist Gerald May that true freedom is not just doing what we want, but being able to do what we *most deeply* want. The reality of saying no to all of the other options available to us, is outweighed by what awaits in a life of saying yes to one person.

So let me extend an invitation to everyone considering marriage, couples old and young, living separately or together: Please keep considering and please keep reading. Read in these pages the wonderful stories of the blessings of sacramental married life—and how full such a life can be. But it is not without risk. There is *no* "safe" path in life. Jesus never promised us that life would be safe. He did promise us a life of joy. And that is what is possible for us all in a life of sacramental marriage.

Why Another Book on Marriage?

With literally thousands of books about marriage on the market, why throw another one onto the pile? I wrote this book primarily because I want to share with you what I wish others had told me about marriage. People told me a lot. Some of it stuck. A lot of it didn't. Most of it was true, but was said in such a way that I couldn't hear it. And while I know everyone had good intentions, the message I kept getting over and over was: "You're young, you don't know what you're getting into, you don't know enough yet, so listen to me because I do." At some point, Mindi and I began tuning it all out and risked making our own way. My hope is that this book will lead you to your own answers.

With this in mind I have been guided by these two principles:

- Share necessary information
- In a practical manner which respects my readers' need for intellectual and emotional autonomy

The information in the forthcoming pages is in areas that are *vital* to healthy relationships—each chapter contains relevant, "must know" information about healthy relating. This information is communicated through the stories of friends, clients with whom I have worked, and my own experience of marriage. At the end of each chapter there is a Scripture meditation with questions for reflection.

This book is not an instruction manual. In as much as there is no instruction manual for life, I believe there can be none for married life. Marriage is an organic, spiritual entity. It defies being boxed in by a foolproof set of steps and directions. Since each marriage is a combination of two unique personalities, it only makes sense that the union of those two individuals will form something unique.

That being said, there are some core areas which need attention in the early years of every marriage. There are practical skills that when applied can help every couple navigate the tumultuous waters of those first years. This book is not a fix-all, nor is it designed to take the place of marriage therapy or marriage preparation courses and programs. It is intended to compliment and enhance those things.

In its pages are the stories of real couples who are working at their marriages, who've opened the door to their lives and allowed me in, to hear and tell their stories—their successes and failures, their joys and sorrows. I hope you recognize that you are not alone, that other couples share your dreams and doubts, hopes and fears, joys and struggles. I pray that as you look into their lives, you find hope and inspiration. I hope the tools and skills presented will be helpful. And most of all, may this be a jumping-off point for you in what will be a lifetime of enriching your marriage.

Crossing the Threshold and Unpacking Our Personal Baggage

After our honeymoon was over, I soon realized that Mindi and I were carrying home more baggage than just our luggage filled with inexpensive Mexican trinkets and cheap rum. In the first few months we began noticing all of our relationships, expectations, and values creeping into our new life together. We had expectations of one another and of life that we had never discussed. We had "issues" we didn't even know about and we began to see aspects of one another's personalities that were just beginning to emerge. It was as if little gremlins were secretly living in our apartment and one by one they began coming out to say "hello."

In the beginning of the movie *Shrek Two*, the newly married ogres, Fiona and Shrek, are discussing an invitation from her parents, the King and Queen of Far Far Away, to return home so that they and the citizens of Far Far Away can meet her new husband and celebrate their marriage. When Shrek refuses to go, they begin to argue. Princess Fiona accuses Shrek of being (surprise, surprise) an ogre. He snaps back that that is exactly what he is and he's not about to *change*—not for anybody. Princess Fiona has the final word though when she reminds Shrek that she has made changes for him: "Think about that, Shrek," she implores. (In case you missed it: In the first movie—Fiona trades in her beautiful human form for green ogredom for the love of Shrek.)

Every husband or wife could testify that there is an "ogre" in our spouse we'd like to change. When that doesn't happen as quickly or in the ways we would like, it is easy to become disappointed and resentful. In the early days of our relationship, my wife kept saying a little mantra: "Women marry men expecting them to change and they don't, while men marry women expecting them not to change and they do!" There is a lot of truth to that statement. Ideally, we marry the person as they are, not for who they could become if they were to change. At the same time, it is foolish to think that nobody changes. We all change to some degree. Our challenge is to accept our spouses when they do change. However, not all changes are healthy or good for a marriage. We're called to support our spouse when the change is authentic, and gently challenge them when it proves otherwise.

There are also those idiosyncrasies that weren't bothersome while we were dating: My "leaving the seat up" was not a huge problem when I visited her house, but after three months of sharing the same bathroom, I suddenly became an inconsiderate "typical man."

Flexibility—The Ninth Beatitude

Flexibility is a difficult virtue to acquire. Most people react to change with some amount of resistance. This is normal and natural. If we never resisted change, we'd never develop a personality. We'd continually remake ourselves into who others want us to be. Too much rigidity, on the other hand, is just as bad. If we never yield, never change, we will find being in relationships very difficult and marriage an impossible undertaking.

Married life will require us to change some of our ways in order to share life with another. As with most things, there is a balance to be struck here. The key to being and staying flexible is moderation. Ideally, in any relationship, married or otherwise, there is a natural give-and-take—a healthy mutual influencing that takes place between spouses. Being flexible allows us to remain true to who we are, yet able to be influenced by our spouse without losing ourselves in the process. Staying engaged in this relational tug-of-war is not easy, but it is an essential task in the first years of marriage.

I like to think of flexibility as the ninth beatitude. "Blessed are the flexible: They shall get along with others." It is tough to be flexible because it runs at odds with our human need for certainty, stability, and security. In our attempts to curb our natural inclinations, con-cupiscence, and original sin we tend toward the extremes of rigid-ity and passivity.

The needs of security, certainty, and stability are all counterparts to our needs for variety, risk, and change. These are all real needs; they are not wants. We each need security in life. We need to know that the sun will come up in the morning. We need to trust that our floors will hold us when we walk on them, our chairs when we sit, our spouses when we marry.

Other needs that we hold in balance are:

Romance and Indifference
Adventure and Familiarity
Intimacy and Isolation
Arousal and Detachment
Companionship and Independence
Spiritual and Secular
Activity and Rest

Work and Play
Security and Risk
Communication and Silence

Our challenge in life, in relationships, and especially in marriage is to balance our competing needs in each of these areas.

Maintaining a sense of humor helps. Laughter has an amazing power to lift the human spirit. It keeps us from taking ourselves too seriously. Being able to laugh at oneself is important in life and essential in marriage.

What's in Your Bags?

Each of us early in life learns ways of being and means of survival in order to make it through life. Our various ways of relating and getting along with others, for good or ill, have gotten us to this point in life. They have made us friends, diminished our anxiety, and helped us to become who we are. Marriage will call for a heightening, shifting, and mellowing of these skills. It will challenge us to learn new skills, improve existing ones, and lay aside others which no longer work for our benefit.

Differences in expressing expectations are integral to married life. Reconciling hidden expectations is part of the adjustment phase in any relationship. Adjusting to life together is not an easy process, but can be an adventure if we are patient and remain open to learning about our spouse and ourselves.

Temptation and Fidelity

Being tempted is not something most couples give much thought to as they are preparing for marriage. It is however, a reality. For various reasons—growing familiarity with each other, lack of communication, unmet sexual needs and unmet emotional needs, and others—spouses are tempted to be unfaithful. In our culture today marital and relational infidelity is becoming increasingly common. With the rise of online dating and social networking and the privacy these things offer, cheating has never been easier.

This is an issue that needs attention in the early years of marriage. I don't suggest having a conversation with your spouse every time you feel tempted. There's usually not much good that comes out of making your spouse your confessor.

Serious temptation or a pattern of serious temptations can indicate that something's amiss. In many marriages affairs happen because one or both spouses are not having some important needs met, spiritually, physically, or emotionally.

It helps to talk about it. But before rushing to your spouse to process these feelings, consider this: Even with masterful communication skills it can be nearly impossible for a spouse to sift through the cobwebs of meaning surrounding the words "I have feelings for someone else," or "I'm becoming increasingly attracted to another person." These types of temptations should be first processed with a priest, trusted spiritual advisor, or professional counselor. These professionals can offer guidance as you sort through your thoughts and feelings, helping lead you to greater awareness and deepened insight around your temptation.

Perhaps the most proactive way to deal with temptation and infidelity is a commitment to continuous, open, honest communication. Ask each other if your needs are being met. One simple way to do this is by asking the question: "On a scale of one to ten, how would you rank me as a spouse?" Once your spouse gives you a number, ask, "What would it take to make it a ten?" The answer to that question is often an unmet need your spouse is currently experiencing. After they answer that question you could then ask,

"What would our relationship look like if I were doing _____?" "What specific things would I be doing differently?" This is not always an easy discussion, but the results, if both of you are honest, can be powerful.

Dealing With Disappointment

In the movie *License to Wed* an idealistic, newly engaged couple, Sadie (Mandy Moore) and Ben (John Krasinski), approach the pastor of her home church, Reverend Frank (Robin Williams), to preside at their wedding. Reverend Frank insists that the couple participate in his "foolproof" marriage preparation program, consisting of classes, homework assignments, and questionable surveillance tactics. Sadie and Ben discover more about one another than they could have imagined, such as how to handle conflict, honesty, sexual issues, and other issues. At one point in the movie it is clear that the image they had of their future spouse has been altered, and both are left disillusioned and disappointed.

Despite the pastor's absurd tactics, the movie offers a realistic view of the issues and challenges couples face, and how easy it would be for these same issues to remain below the surface until after the wedding. Ben and Sadie were fortunate to be able to learn of their differences at an early stage. More often than not, couples do not glean such insights into one another until after the honeymoon.

In every marriage, there comes a sobering awareness that you are not able to do as much of your own thing. Even with a great marriage preparation experience, it is still normal for couples to wake up one day and think, "This is not the person I married. What happened?" It is natural for couples to experience some disillusionment in the early years. A time comes when you realize that your spouse isn't all you thought and things aren't working out quite as smoothly as you once hoped. In his book *Against an Infinite Horizon*, Father Ronald Rolheiser captures this phase perfectly:

> ...the sadness, longing, and disappointment ultimately originate not from the fact that love has not taken place, but that human love is finite. This insight helps us realize that the first task in any love, whether in a marriage or in a deep friendship, is for the two persons to console each other for the limits of their love, for the fact that they cannot not disappoint each other.[1]

We were not created to bear the weight of perfection. Let us be content to be who God made us—broken, imperfect beings. In marriage we face the ever present challenge to love one another despite our brokenness and many shortcomings.

Celebrating the Sacrament

The primary purpose of the sacraments is to transmit God's grace. Grace is not something we earn by being good Christians. It is God's free gift to us. Once married we face the challenging task of melding our individual self with another—two whole, complete people coming together for a greater purpose. Remaining whole and complete while merging with another to form something new is only possible with the help of God's grace. This grace is available to us through the sacramentality of our marriage.

One evening I was venting about a work situation to a friend over the phone. I was throwing myself a verbal pity party, and in a roundabout way going on and on about out how important I was and how disrespected I felt. I was acting like a spoiled, entitled child. After my conversation ended I could tell Mindi was upset, so

I asked why. "Listening to you really stressed me out. You were screaming into the phone and threatening to leave your job. I mean, that's not who you are. That's not you at all."

What I wanted to hear was, "Honey, you are so important. You deserve to be treated better than that. I can't believe they're not bending over backward to make you happy. How dare they not acquiesce to your every whim." That is what I wanted. What I *needed* was for her to say exactly what she did. How did I react? I went straight into the living room, sat on the couch and sulked. After five minutes my inflated, bruised ego knew she was right. Mindi was gracious enough to take the initiative by coming to sit beside me and assuring me of how much she loved me, and while it pained her to see my feelings hurt she felt it necessary to challenge me to higher ground. I then apologized.

None of us is perfect. We're all a mixed bag. Inside each of us coexists light and darkness, good and bad, grace and sin. Ideally, sacramental marriage is a safe place where we can be confronted on our "stuff." Left to our own natural devices, our first and only reaction would be to fortify our ego, stand our ground and be right. Grace enables a relationship to transcend our natural inclinations. Grace can transform what would otherwise be a convenient living arrangement into a sacred space where we feel safe enough to expose our brokenness and receive forgiveness.

Marriage is not for the faint of heart. It will call upon all of your existing resources and require you to find more. It requires courage to remain committed to a relationship when it seems easier to bail. On our own, it would be a no-brainer. It would make sense to check out and disengage. But in a covenantal relationship we are not alone. God's spirit lives in and among us. A husband and wife can offer God's grace to one another like no other relationship can.

In married love, husbands and wives serve as conduits of God's grace to each other, their children, and the world. This is no small thing. In their pastoral letter *Follow the Way of Love,* the U.S. bishops say that the purpose of marriage and family life is ultimately union with God:

> Your family life is sacred because family relationships confirm and deepen this union and allow the Lord to work through you. The profound and the ordinary moments of daily life—mealtimes, workdays, vacations, expressions of love and intimacy, household chores, caring for a sick child or elderly parent, and even conflicts over things like how to celebrate holidays, discipline children, or spend money— are all threads from which you can weave a pattern of holiness. [2]

We don't just become holy as individuals. As part of God's design, we live and move among others. God has chosen to transform the world through the grace, love, and witness of a married couple and their family.

The sacramental grace that God makes available in marriage is more than simply a gift to a husband and wife. It is also God's gift to the world.

Marriage reveals the mysterious nature of God's love. Married love reveals to us in some sense the nature of our Trinitarian God and something about our God's love for us, his most precious creation. In his first papal encyclical, *Deus Caritas Est*, Pope Benedict XVI addresses the meaning of love (*eros*) in our lives. He writes:

> From the standpoint of creation, eros directs man towards marriage, to a bond which is unique and definitive; thus,

and only thus, does it fulfil [sic] its deepest purpose. …Marriage based on exclusive and definitive love becomes the icon of the relationship between God and his people and vice versa. God's way of loving becomes the measure of human love.[3]

Surrendering to Freedom

My bachelor party was a night I'll always remember. Whereas lots of guys go to strip clubs and that sort of thing, we were elated to fry a turkey, braise deer meat, and barbeque pork tenderloin. I had been looking forward to it for months. When we had arrived, no sooner had I stepped out of the car than a bottle of bourbon was shoved into my chest (looking back, clearly it was more of a diversionary tactic than a sign of love) and two of my groomsmen were wrapping a chain around my right leg with my grandmother's old, beat up, black bowling ball attached to the end. The idiots had duct taped a sheet of paper to it that said "Mindi."

"You've got to be kidding me!" I yelled, feeling the sting of the chain as it bit into my ankle when trying to move. Despite my repeated pleas to cut it off of my leg, it remained attached to me for the entire night until I woke up the next morning.

This image has become a real symbol of marriage for many in my generation. It assumes that by making a lifelong commitment we will somehow lose who we are in the process, and become a slave to another person and one relationship. Nothing could be further from the truth.

For years I enjoyed doing whatever I wanted to do, going where I wanted, when I wanted. And that was a wonderful and *necessary* season of my life. But, it grew old. There came a time when always having fun lost its appeal. I remember feeling in the words of the popular song, "There's gotta be something more." I didn't know exactly what that *more* was back then but I sensed that I wanted more from me and more from life. My spirit, my soul, instead of growing as it once had, was becoming stagnant.

Real freedom, I began to sense, did not mean keeping all of my options open, but rather having the inner freedom to choose one woman, amidst all others, commit to one way of life in lieu of other options. I was learning what psychiatrist and spiritual author Gerald May meant when he said that freedom, although seen by many as the ability to do whatever we want, is really "the ability to do what we most deeply want." I knew that what I most deeply wanted was to love and be loved—by God and another human being. If marriage was indeed a forum for that to happen then that's what I wanted. In that sense marriage, rather than revoking my freedom, delivered me to it in ways I had never imagined.

Scripture: Genesis 2:20–24

The man gave names to all cattle, and to the birds of the air, and to every animal of the field; but for the man there was not found a helper as his partner. So the Lord God caused a deep sleep to fall upon the man, and he slept; then he took one of his ribs and closed up its place with flesh. And the rib that the Lord God had taken from the man he made into a woman and brought her to the man. Then the man said,

"This at last is bone of my bones
and flesh of my flesh;
this one shall be called Woman,
for out of Man this one was taken."

Therefore a man leaves his father and his mother and clings to his wife, and they become one flesh.

For Reflection

1. What adjustments were most difficult early in your marriage? What adjustments do you anticipate being difficult? How might you prepare for them?

2. What expectations did/do you have about marriage? How has the reality of marriage differed from what you expected?

3. What has been most gratifying in your marriage/relationship so far? What has been the most disappointing?

4. Is a loss of freedom something that is a concern for you?

5. What has been some of the "baggage" you brought into your relationship? How have you handled your respective baggage?

Can You Hear Me Now? Communicating as Husband and Wife

One day Mindi and I were sitting next to each other in the waiting room of a doctor's office. I reached in my pocket for my phone in order to send her a text message about someone's hairstyle across the room. You ever have one of those moments when, as it is happening, you realize that it is special or significant? This was one of those moments. I figured it was worth capturing in text: "I can't believe we're texting each other and our shoulders are touching. Wow."

Each day there are 2.5 billion text messages sent by nearly 263 million American wireless subscribers. Not counting other modes of telecommunication such as e-mail, it is safe to conclude that communication has never been easier. Never has the average person been able to be more connected and more accessible. You'd think this would make us *better* at communication. But researchers at the University of Creighton in their study "Time, Sex and Money" report that communication is one of the major problematic issues faced by couples in their first few years.

Tuning In

When I was a kid, I remember how hard it was to catch a station on my mom's car radio. It had a big silver dial that you would turn through the station numbers listening for your station to come in clearly. If you turned too fast you'd miss the station signal. You had to slowly turn and then perhaps wiggle the dial to get it exactly right in order to get a clear signal. I was always frustrated because I'd somehow turn just past it, losing the signal. Communication in a relationship can be just as trying.

Mike and Beth have been married for fifteen years. Mike is an outgoing, analytical, intellectual type while Beth is reserved and emotional. In their case opposites did indeed attract. After a long week of him working and her at home caring for their three children, they went on a date. Beth enjoyed these times with Mike, because she could be the object of his focused attention. She didn't have to compete with the kids, the TV, or computer games. Her only competition this night was the menu.

Once they were seated for dinner, Mike asked Beth to tell him about her week. Beth began chronicling her struggles with the kids, being behind on housework, and the other frustrations experienced by so many moms who work in the home. She noticed, not for the first time, that Mike had drifted off and wasn't listening. She decided to have a little fun and test Mike to see exactly how "tuned out" he was to what she was saying. "In mid-conversation I just started saying ridiculous things like 'The house is burning down,' 'The waitress is holding a flaming cat!,' 'A masked man just walked through the door and is waving a gun through the air.' Mike's eyes remained glazed over staring out the window while nodding and mumbling 'Uh huh.' I just started crying and managed to squeeze in between sobs 'You're-not-list-e-ning-to me,'" Beth says today with a half smile.

Listening is difficult, but it is vital to effective communication. Most problems in communication can be solved by practicing the techniques of effective listening.

The first step in tuning in is to become mindful of the fact that you need to be listening to your partner. One of the deepest human needs is to be understood. When we feel heard, deeply listened to, we feel connected and loved.

It is common for couples to grow complacent in their communication skills. At some point spouses, albeit unconsciously, develop a perception that they know one another already. The problem with this reasoning is that we box in or limit our spouse. When we feel that we know one another, as if it is a one-time event, we unconsciously limit their ability to grow. We are always changing and growing.

Listening is a skill that can be learned. And while some pick up this skill through watching their parents and others around them, for most people good listening skills must be intentionally learned and practiced. And we need to learn them if we want to have rich relationships. The following are some basic skills of active listening:

- *Sit up straight.* If someone walked into your home holding a check for $5 million with your name on it, I'd bet they'd have your attention. And if they said, "Before I give you this check I need to give you specific directions about how to cash it," what would you do? You'd sit up straight. You'd be hanging on to their every syllable not wanting to miss any piece of information needed to cash in your $5 million. Sitting up straight sends a signal to our brains to pay attention and not drift off. It also communicates respect for the speaker. Your marriage is worth more than $5 million.

- *Make and keep eye contact.* It has been said that eyes are the windows to the soul. By facing one another, maintaining and keeping eye contact, we communicate that we really do want to understand. It signals that we care so much about what is being said that we want to see what we cannot hear with our ears. Only a small portion of what we communicate to others happens through our words.

• *Ask clarifying questions.* This serves two purposes: One, it assures accuracy of understanding and two, it tells the listener that you really are trying to understand.

• *Nod or make a vocal noise like "uh-huh" to communicate that you are following what they are saying.* These let the speaker know you are listening and understand what they are saying without interrupting them.

• *Don't interrupt.* Don't interrupt unless it's to gain clarity. Your effective listening will do more for the communication process than any argument you may fail to introduce, because you couldn't remember to bring it up when it was your turn.

• *Reflect back your understanding of what is being said.* This is when you communicate back to the listener what you believe they are saying. You may say, "Let's see if I understand the points you are making…"

• *Ask "Do you feel heard?"* Once we've said what we think is being said we give the speaker the opportunity to acknowledge our efforts and effectiveness at listening and comprehension. If they say yes, at the beginning you may want to ask, "In what ways specifically do you feel deeply heard?" If they say no, then you can ask, "What am I missing?"

• *Close with "Is there anything else you'd like to say?"* This says, "I'm with you so far, but since it's your turn to talk, you get to make as many points as you need." This can go a long way to bridging the communication divide.

• *Reserve the right to postpone the conversation.* When we know that we are distracted and cannot offer our undivided attention, we might say something like, "I can't give you my full attention right now, but I want to. Is there any way we might talk about this at another time? If so, what time would be best for you?" This substantially decreases the potential for unnecessary conflict.

Practicing these techniques may feel awkward at first, but that feeling will lessen with time. Practicing these skills will ease conversational tension, lower resistance, and create greater openness and receptivity.

Beyond the Golden Rule

I'm not sure whether it was the tenth or the twentieth time that I tried to cook a five-star meal for my wife in a vain attempt to show her my love that the conversation during the meal sounded a little like this:

> "How do you like your steak?" (Translation: I paid $15 for that piece of meat to tell you that I love you. Please like it!)
> "It's good, baby." (Translation: It's OK, but it's not lighting my world on fire).
> "What? You don't like it?" (Translation: Why on earth would your world not light up over a choice rib-eye steak that I slaved to prepare for you?)
> "No, it's good, babe, I like it." (Translation: What I would love is to sit on the couch with a glass of wine and talk, go dancing or for a long walk in the park).

Two years into our marriage I believed that I was performing an amazing act of love by exerting tons of effort to prepare a five-star meal—this all for a woman who eats only because she must. While I live to eat, my wife, Mindi, eats in order to live. My attempts at showing her love with food were at first noble and thoughtful gestures of my love, and she regarded them as such. But one can only feign satisfaction for so long.

Mindi, on the other hand, seemed to think she was showing her love for me by spending great amounts of time with me and giving me neck massages. In a similar way, I accepted her loving gestures in the generous spirit with which they were offered. It soon became clear that we were both tolerating the other's attempt to communicate love, and were not hitting the bull's-eye. And while we had not come to the end of our rope, we were realizing that we were not making one another feel as special as we once did with the same tried and true gestures.

Most people are familiar with the Golden Rule which says, "Do unto others as you would have them do unto you" (Luke 6:31). In marriage, however, the Golden Rule falls short. Often we don't want to be treated the way our spouse likes to be treated. We all want to be treated the way *we* want to be treated. Effective communicating and relating understands that inside of most people is a desire that says, "Do unto me as I would have you do unto me."

God has designed us with an emotional filter. Amid the many messages of love and affection we receive every day, there are one or two primary ways we tend to receive this love. The challenge is to recognize our own dominant love language(s) and those of our spouse. And then to begin showing them love in the way *they* want to be loved. In his book, *The Five Love Languages*, Doctor Gary Chapman describes five different ways we both express and receive love. I have tried to summarize these ways below:

- *Words of affirmation*—People who require these will tend to experience love through verbal praise, recognition, and gratitude. They enjoy compliments, hearing appreciation, acknowledgment of their uniqueness or what makes them special. They are especially sensitive to words of encouragement.

- *Quality time*—People who require this feel and experience love by receiving all of another person's attention and focus during a set period of time. Quality time is defined as being more than being close to one another. It means that we give our spouse our concentrated, focused attention. We can spend time alone with our spouse or loved one without ever experiencing quality time with them. Self-revelation is an essential aspect of quality time love. It requires that we are in touch with our own emotional life and are growing in the freedom to share and express that with another.

- *Receiving gifts*—People who require gifts see them as symbols of another person's love for us. This is the easiest love language to learn. This can be, however, difficult for someone who does not like spending money. The challenge for this person will be to grow in their awareness that it is not about wasting money, but it is a concrete symbol and expression of their love for their spouse. The gifts do not need to be expensive or overly frequent. Simple, thoughtful gifts express to the other that we have thought enough about them to recognize and purchase a gift for them.

- *Acts of service*—People who require acts of service, such as performing everyday chores or errands, need clarification about what types of service our spouse most appreciates. For example, I know I need my clothes washed and dried, but I feel very special when Mindi takes the time to cook supper and do the dishes afterward. I know that she has gone out of her way to do something she ordinarily does not like to do, in order to express love to me. This can be difficult for individuals when it requires them to commit acts of service that may not typically be inclined to (or like to) perform.

• *Physical touch*—Most people in married relationships require physical touch. Sexual intercourse tends to be a powerful way of experiencing love, affection, intimacy, and security. Both sensual touch and nonsensual touching are extremely powerful expressions of affection. Again, just as in acts of service, this too requires clarity. We must learn what types of touch are most appreciated by our spouse. Sometimes it is a back massage, others a hug or a simple cheek caress. [1]

The Power of Making an Effective Request

When I was young and I didn't get what I wanted from my mom, I hung out my bottom lip and pouted. Asking directly for what we wanted was not practiced in my family. Indirect or passive-aggressive attempts at getting one's way were honored, while aggressive or explicit ways were frowned upon.

As I grew older I noticed my passive attempts at getting attention or other things I wanted or needed were not working very well. Behaviors once tolerated and even rewarded in my family were not making me many friends. I was fortunate to be around people who loved me enough to challenge me, and invite me into healthier ways of relating. I was given opportunities to learn a more healthy and effective way of meeting my needs. I learned how to make requests of other people.

There are two primary types of requests most often made in marriage.

A specific request: "Honey, can you go to the store and pick up some milk this afternoon?" That is an isolated event. The person being asked can either say yes or no to this request based upon desire or availability to do that specific thing.

General requests: This is the classic case of the left-up toilet seat. "Honey, whenever (every time) you go to use the restroom, please (always) raise the seat and when you are finished (always) put it back down." This is a request for a behavior that is to be repeated over and over. General requests can be more tricky because they may involve character issues. These can be difficult to formulate because they tend to be very direct and seem confrontational. Whenever you catch yourself making a generalization about your spouse, that's a clue that what you really want is to make a general request. For example, "You are such as stingy person," might be formulated as a request by saying, "Honey, I would like to discuss being more generous in our tithing to the church. Can we do that? If so, what would be a good time for you?" In the case of Mike and Beth, Beth was able to ask Mike, "Honey, whenever we go out on a date, I would like to request that you make a concerted effort to pay attention to what I am saying."

Two other important considerations when making requests are:

1. Gain assurance that the listener understands exactly what you are requesting.
2. Ask them if they are willing to grant your request.

Like all "skills" this at first may seem forced and awkward. I can say that today this skill has become second nature for Mindi and me. Often we'll catch one another being passive or complaining and ask, "Is there something you want to ask of me?" Doing this prevents the build up of resentments that can easily creep into a relationship.

When to Talk, and When Not to

I'm a talker. Mindi is not. I cannot think without my mouth moving. She needs quiet time alone to gather her thoughts in order to speak. You can already see where this is going. When problems come up in our relationship, I want to start hashing it out right away. My motto: The sooner we start talking it out, the sooner it'll be over.

Mindi's motto: Sit on it for at least a little while, and once we both cool off and think it through, we'll have something non-reactive and productive to say. She needs time to think about what the issues are and how she *really* feels about them. And then, come up with words to express those feelings. Words don't come as easily to her as they do to me.

You can see my dilemma. In my mind, everything needs to be talked about. In many respects we are just beginning to honor each other needs when it comes to processing issues and conflict. I'm learning to be patient while she figures it out, and she's learning to honor my need for verbal processing of the issues involved. We are both committed to finding a solution regardless of how much talking it takes or quiet time it takes.

Determine when a good time to talk is—and when it is not. I've learned in my own relationship and by looking into those of friends and clients that sometimes it's best not to talk right away. Some things are better left unsaid, and some things need time on the shelf so that when they are said, they will be spoken in the right way.

When asked what advice they would give young couples, the couples interviewed in the Creighton study on the first five years of marriage, said: "Communicate, communicate, communicate." It would seem that it is better to overcommunicate than under communicate. I once read a sign that said, "That which goes unspoken controls the relationship." It's too easy to sweep things under the rug hoping they'll just go away. The truth is that they don't. They lie in wait only to pop up later on with even more intensity.

As uncomfortable as it may be, it is better to deal with issues directly and in a timely manner.

Scripture: James 1:19–21

You must understand this, my beloved: let everyone be quick to listen, slow to speak, slow to anger; for your anger does not produce God's righteousness. Therefore rid yourselves of all sordidness and rank growth of wickedness, and welcome with meekness the implanted word that has the power to save your souls.

For Reflection

1. What makes it difficult to tune in and listen to your spouse?
2. Which communication skills are you most proficient at? Which ones need work?
3. What are your top two love languages? What are those of your spouse? In what ways do you speak to one another's dominant language?
4. What boundaries have you needed to establish so far? Which do you still need to establish?
5. What is an example of one request you have made so far? What situations come to mind that might have been diffused more easily by making an effective request?

CHAPTER THREE

Time: The Real Amazing Race

Creighton University's Center for Marriage and Family in their research on couples who were in their first five years of marriage found that the most problematic issue was balancing time spent among their various commitments. Time is our most precious resource. How we spend our time is how we spend our lives.

Time Is Not the Problem

Time management is one of the most talked about subjects today. Everybody seems to want to make the most of his or her time. Some experts have suggested that a lack of time is our problem. I disagree. Time is not the problem. We are.

For decades now we've blamed time and tried to manage it. Time rolls by at the same pace every day, for everybody. God gives us all twenty-four hours in a day. It's up to us what we do with those twenty-four hours. What is lacking is not an ability to manage time, but the ability to manage our priorities. Priority management is choice management, because we make our choices based upon our priorities.

Identifying Priorities

We all have priorities. Priorities guide every decision we make. If I eat two or three doughnuts every day, even though my doctor has warned me about my elevated cholesterol, then I value the pleasure and satisfaction that eating those doughnuts gives me. I might also claim to have made "being in good health" a priority, but when faced with the choice of doughnuts versus good health, choosing to eat the doughnuts reveals which is a higher priority for me. One easy way to recognize our priorities is to examine our choices. Our track record of choices reveals what we value most.

When we aren't aware of what our priorities are, it is impossible to follow through on them *consistently*. It is that consistent living in alignment with the values and beliefs that are most important to us that gives us a sense of control, peace, and happiness. It doesn't matter whether or not our to-do list is five pages long and we only get two things on that list done. At the end of the day what will matter is that they were the *top* two things on the list.

Identifying priorities can be a confusing process. Even knowing where to begin can seem like finding a needle in a haystack. If you live a busy life juggling many important commitments, it may seem as though everything is important.

Here is a simple process that will help you gain clarity around your priorities.

Step One: Carve out a half hour where you can be alone and quiet. Get a sheet of paper. I find that writing things down forces me to look at things the way they are, whereas when left in my head I can make them into what I want them to be. Begin listing the things, commitments, people, obligations, values that are important to you. Resist your tendency to edit this as you write. Now is not the time to edit, rank, and evaluate. If playing with pick up sticks is important to you, or you really like to do it, write it down. If eating right and exercising is important to you, write it down. If later you change your mind, then you can scratch it off the list. But for now, write everything down.

Step Two: Begin assigning a numerical rank to each item on your list. Number one is your highest priority, number two, second highest and so on. This is very difficult. It is hard because it forces us to decide among really good and important things. It forces us to *decide* that item A is more important than item B. When we make this decision and see it on paper, it forces us to acknowledge the ways we are not living in accord with our most important values and priorities.

Below is a list of my priorities in no particular order:

- Career
- God
- Family
- Friends
- Hobbies
- Physical health
- Mental/emotional health
- Leisure time
- Continued learning
- Cooking

OK, this is a sample short list. These are the things I like to do the most. As you can probably tell, several of these categories could easily be broken down into subcategories and perhaps divided even further. But for the sake of this exercise we'll keep it simple. Usually, this is what my list looks like when I'm done prioritizing:

1. Physical health
2. God/spiritual life
3. Family
4. Career/writing
5. Friends/social life
6. Mental/emotional health
7. Continued learning
8. Hobbies
9. Cooking
10. Leisure time

Remember, this is *my* list. It is not meant to be *the* list. The important thing in this exercise is that we are honest. It does no good to arrange our priorities the way we think our spouse wants to hear them or the way we think they should be.

Tracking Time

Another powerful exercise is to track your time. For one week keep track of how you spend your time. Twice a day log what it is you do, and how long it took you to do it. There's an old saying, "Show me your checkbook and your calendar and I'll tell you what your priorities are."

This may be a very eye-opening experience. As we look back over the past week at how we spent our time, perhaps we will notice that we spent great amounts of time doing things that were not aligned with our highest priorities. Everyone does this to some extent. The challenge is to minimize the time we spend off track. Resist the urge to be overly critical and instead use this as an opportunity for improvement. Becoming aware of the incongruence between what we value and how we spend our time can be a big motivation to refocus and realign.

Getting In Sync

This is a great exercise to do as a couple. Once each of you has completed the individual exercise, come together and discuss your results. This can be a very powerful exercise in communication and connection. In the midst of the daily grind, it is difficult for this kind of connecting to happen. Business and a calendar full of commitments keep us floating along the surface, if for no other reason than it takes too much time to dive in and come back up, so we resist plunging down deep on a regular basis to connect on a soul level.

Just as in the individual exercise, create some time, away from the kids, turn off the TV, silence the cell phones, perhaps pour a glass of wine (or coffee depending on what time of day it is) and begin sharing your lists of priorities. Try not to be judgmental toward your spouse's priorities. Sitting in judgment over what's deeply important to your spouse is a recipe for disaster. Try to see this as an opportunity to explore and learn about your partner. Ask probing questions, such as, "Can you tell me more about that?" and then give them an opportunity to expand upon their choices, rather than *defend* their choices. Use this time as an opportunity to celebrate what you share in common and gently explore your differences.

When I lead people through this exercise, they'll spend most of their time discussing their top three to five priorities. After sharing your individual lists, consider creating a small list as a couple. What are five values, or areas of your relationship that you both consider to be important? This does not need to be a one-time event. In fact it's best if you revisit this list again and again throughout the course of your relationship. Over the years items on that list may change, and they may increase or decrease in importance. What will matter is that you are both aware of what's on the list.

When we begin identifying and acting on the things, commitments, and values that matter most to us, we build momentum and a sense of confidence. Our living takes on greater intentionality and purpose—two things that give us as an individual and as a couple greater peace and satisfaction.

Staying In Sync

Only one year after the birth of their first child, Cindy and Mark found themselves in the all too common situation of trying to handle too much, too quickly. They each knew they were too busy, and needed to come together to talk about their schedule, but like so many young families, they were so busy that one day just rolled into the next and the talk never happened.

They decided to institute a weekly meeting. Once a week they sat together for a time of extended prayer and planning. "We light a candle, pray, and look at our schedules for the days, weeks, and months ahead. It's simple, and that's why I think it works. It's become our family 'in box,' a place where we can dump all of the stuff that can be put on hold for a few days, which is a lot, but still need our focused attention as a couple," says Cindy.

They immediately noticed the benefits. Mark noted, "After the first meeting we felt less stressed out. I guess it was because we felt like, after having looked at everything out in the open, we had a sense of control. Combine that with a time of prayer and asking for God's guidance in our life, we started looking forward to our Sunday meeting because of the sense of peace and purpose it gave us."

For Mark and Cindy taking thirty minutes once a week to sort through the "stuff" of their life saved them hours in running around, making unnecessary phone calls, sending unnecessary e-mails and most importantly, creating unnecessary conflict by a lack of systematic, effective communication.

Sunday afternoons while their son takes a nap works for them, but any time can work as long as it is a quiet protected time. That means no kids, phones, and if possible, distractions. Below is a rough outline of their family meeting:

Step One: Prayer
(This will be covered in detail in chapter nine.)

Step Two: Review Goals
Goals can be roughly divided into three broad areas: what, when, and who. What we want to have, when we want to do things, and who we want to be. You can divide them any way you'd like; this worked for us.

- *What (material)*—These include what type of house you may want, where you would like to live, what type of car you want to drive—all the "stuff" that's in life that you would like or need. This includes any items that might need to be repaired or updated. Consider this a dream list. Don't overly scrutinize what goes onto it—if you want it, write it. You can always scratch it off later.
- *When (to dos)*—This is where you pull out the calendars, both personal and family. Look at the week ahead, compare schedules, and evaluate requests for your time and things that need to get done. Then look over the month ahead, major commitments you have made and would like to make. Finally, glance over the year. What big things would you like to do or accomplish in the next year (together or individually)? Things such as vacation, trips and retreats would come up here. And remember, it's just a plan. You can change it next week.

- *Who (personal goals)*—Because these things tend to be personal and a bit vague, they often go unvoiced. That is unfortunate because these, not the calendar or material items, are the heart of any relationship. When you risk sharing dreams and hopes both as individuals and as a couple you create a powerful opportunity for connection. Questions that help guide this type of sharing might be: What kind of person do you want to be? What do you want people to say about your relationship? What gift might your marriage and family be to the world? What type of parents do you want to be? What type of life do you envision for yourself in the years to come?

Most people have some sort of personal time management device, whether it is paper based or digital (PDAs, etc.). But how do you know what's on your spouse's calendar? As busy people we're constantly evaluating requests for our time and making commitments. Staying in sync with each other in marriage can be very difficult without a plan in place.

A family organizing device can be as simple or as complex as you need it to be. Sam and Denise have found the simpler the better works for them. For years they've functioned well by using the sticking-the-church-calendar-to-the-refrigerator method. To some modern ears this might sound laughably simple. But it works! What makes it work is that it possesses what I believe are the three keys to an effective calendar system:

1. They understand it. They don't need manuals or tutorials to help them use it.

2. They trust it. The most sophisticated system in the world won't work if you don't trust it to track your commitments. When you have a system you don't trust, you end up second guessing it and using it sporadically. Inevitably important things will fall through the cracks.
3. They use it. No system will work if you don't use it. Everything has to go on the calendar in order for it to work.

I have other friends who are more tech-savvy and prefer to use digital calendars. They cite the advantages being that they can print out a hard copy whenever they wish, yet maintain the ease and maneuverability that comes with a digital planner. The main advantage of digital planners is that they can now be synced by phone or online, enabling them to meet the above-mentioned criteria for an effective planning system. If a shared family calendar doesn't seem doable for you, just make sure that you and your spouse visit frequently with your individual calendars to prevent over commitment and scheduling conflicts.

Another aspect of staying in sync is deciding which issues need discussion and which can be made on an individual basis. Decide if it's OK for one of you to make social commitments without consulting the other. How much notice would you like in advance? Addressing this issue will inevitably save you time sorting through conflicts later on.

It's Just an Empty Cup

In the motion picture *Cars*, Lighting McQueen, the young, brash, famous race car is obsessed with winning the Piston Cup, racing's highest honor. He is sure that winning this cup will lock his place in history and merit him a lucrative sponsorship. In a foolish attempt to beat his fellow competitors to the final race, he ends up in a small town amidst people who have never heard of him, who simply want him to fix the road he came in on and then leave on it.

While in Radiator Springs, Lighting befriends several of the natives and discovers that Doc, the town judge and father figure, is a former racing legend who had won three Piston Cups in his day, but had kept it a secret from the town. When Lighting could not understand why Doc wasn't showcasing his trophies, Doc retorts, "It's just an empty cup."

When we fail to make time to identify and prioritize what's most important to us, we risk rushing through life, chasing an empty cup.

As we begin to reflect on God's gift of time and our use of it, we will grow in awareness of what's truly important and give ourselves the chance of living lives in alignment with those priorities.

Scripture: Ecclesiastes 3:1–8

For everything there is a season, and a time for every matter under heaven:

a time to be born, and a time to die;
a time to plant, and a time to pluck up what is planted;
a time to kill, and a time to heal;
a time to break down, and a time to build up;
a time to weep, and a time to laugh;
a time to mourn, and a time to dance;
a time to throw away stones, and a time to gather stones together;
a time to embrace, and a time to refrain from embracing;
a time to seek, and a time to lose;
a time to keep, and a time to throw away;

a time to tear, and a time to sew;

a time to keep silence, and a time to speak;

a time to love, and a time to hate;

a time for war, and a time for peace.

For Reflection

1. Make a list of people, things, and values that are important to you. Take the time to rank them in order of their importance. Is the importance of each item reflected in the amount of time you spend on it?

2. What are some things you could begin doing differently with your time? What are some things you can stop doing?

3. Where does personal prayer and prayer as a couple fit into your busy life? What keeps you from making and taking time for this? How comfortable are you with praying with your spouse?

4. What decisions regarding time commitments need to be made as a couple and which can be made as individuals?

CHAPTER FOUR

You Complete Me: Sex and the Christian Marriage

In the first couple of years of their marriage, Kristen and Jeff had a very active and healthy sex life. At some point in their third year of marriage they began having sex less frequently. They knew that most couples experience some drop off in their sexual frequency after marriage, but soon they noticed they were having sex on average less than once a week. They never addressed the issue.

One afternoon after having sex, as was his custom, Jeff leaned over and asked Kristen if she enjoyed sex and if she had achieved orgasm. At first Kristen said "yes." But then she said, "Well, actually, no, I didn't." When Jeff asked her to explain why she at first said yes, she said, "I faked it."

What happened between Kristen and Jeff? How did they go from sex three times per week to less than once a week and then lying about sexual gratification? What changed? The better question to ask is, "What didn't happen?" The answer to that question is at the heart of many sexual problems experienced by couples: open and honest communication.

Talking About Sex

In nearly fifteen years of youth ministry I believe that of the hundreds of teens I worked with, most of them had their first conversation about sex with me. Many people don't like to talk about sex.

In many cultures the subject of sex is taboo. And like most taboos, people avoid speaking about them as it is against the cultural norms. You would think that in a society that sends shows like *Sex and the City* to the top of the ratings charts, we would be long separated from such inhibitions. And while some people are comfortable talking about sex, many couples list their sex life as one of the areas in which they experience the least satisfaction in their marriage.

Body Image

Today as Jeff looks back he attributes much of their communication problems about sex to his own pervasive negative body image. As a kid he struggled with his physical appearance. Even after growing out of much of what he disliked about his appearance that negative image followed him into adulthood. For many men and women, even feeling slightly overweight, underweight, feeling as if they are too short or too tall or unattractive can create distorted and unhealthy body images. As we see in Jeff and Kristen's story, such issues left untended can creep into the bedroom and begin affecting a once vibrant sex life.

This issue is especially insidious for women today. God endowed women with a deep need to feel beautiful. As John and Stasi Eldredge in their book *Captivating*, write,

> Beauty is what the world longs to experience from a woman. We know that. Somewhere down deep, we know it to be true. Most of our shame comes from this knowing and feeling that we have failed here...beauty is an essence that dwells in every woman. It was given to her by God.

> Beauty is the most essential and, yes, the most misunderstood of all the feminine qualities…The only things standing in the way of our beauty are our doubts and fears…[1]

Beauty is a complex combination of inner and outer qualities. This understanding about beauty stands in sharp contrast to that of our modern American culture which often glorifies computer enhanced images of women who are dangerously thin.

In addition to issues of body image, another reason talking about sex is difficult is that it requires us to overcome centuries of conditioning in which sex has been portrayed as something which is dirty and bad. Part of this stems from a misinterpretation of Saint Paul's use of the word "flesh." In his letter to the Romans, Paul says "…those who are in the flesh cannot please God." Over the years many well-intended preachers have used this passage to exhort the faithful to avoid immoral sexual behavior. And certainly that is part of what Paul is suggesting here. But, it is a small part. Paul's concept of flesh is our wounded human nature, which is susceptible to temptation. When Saint Paul uses the word "flesh" in this instance he uses the Greek word *sarx* in the original letter, and is referring to disordered human desires. If he were talking about our skin and our bodies, he would have used the Greek word *soma*.

Our bodies, our sexuality, and sexual intercourse are all gifts from God. As such they are *holy*. As with all of God's gifts, sex is to be enjoyed in its proper context, within the sacrament of marriage.

The reality is that most couples spend the first few years of their marriage working out the problems in their sex lives. Adjusting to the nuances in one another's bodies, moods, and sexual signals takes time. This is why you need to speak openly and honestly about what's working and what's not, and expectations of frequency.

Distorted theological perspectives on "flesh" and bodily insecurities are not the only inhibitors of communicating about sex.

Other things that make it difficult to talk about sex are:

- *Trauma from sexual assault or abuse.* In many cases, these events are traumatic for their victims. There may be a resistance to talking about sex, for fear of triggering painful memories of the trauma.
- *Sense of guilt.* For some, communication about sex when they were young was laden with guilt. Sex is God's gift to a husband and wife, and God wants to free you of this unfounded guilt in order to fully experience and enjoy his gift.
- *Anxiety.* This is fairly common. Because sex holds such power it is only natural to experience some anxiety and embarrassment before talking about it.
- *Perfectionism and frustration.* When there are problems in your sex life, it's normal for men to experience frustration with themselves due to a perceived sense of inadequacy. It is good to talk about the frustration. It can be very powerful for a man to experience warmth, love, and acceptance after sharing this.
- *Fear of blame.* Perhaps you've tried talking about sex and slipped into the blame game. While this is normal, the spouse who shoulders the blame may be carrying shame and responsibility for problems in your sex life.

In light of these and other issues you may wish to consider the following tips for making talking about sex easier and less intimidating:

- *Start with prayer.* Prayer reminds us that our bodies, sexuality, and our sex life are God's gifts to us. Ask God for humility, openness, and tenderness. Starting here elevates the discourse, and frames sex in its proper place.

• *Use scientific names for genitals.* Growing up we learned "pet" names for our private parts. As adults it can feel awkward to use the scientific nomenclature. But if you use the words more often when talking about sex, it will make the whole experience of sex talk less embarrassing.

• *Be gentle.* This is a good rule of thumb in all marital discourse, but especially important in this area. Assume that your spouse is sensitive about this issue and be gentle when expressing problems.

• *Be clear.* Being gentle means that we use softer tones and words. It does not mean that we avoid the issue. Address whatever problems that exist directly. Make sure that you each understand what the problem is.

• *Ask questions.* When we ask questions we are showing that we genuinely want to work on the issue. This communicates profound respect and love for your spouse.

How Often?

How much and how often? Most married couples find that each other's sexual needs vary—one partner may feel the need for sex every night, another may be content to forgo sex for days or weeks at a time. Either way, it is an issue to address before and during marriage. In his first letter to the Corinthians Paul encourages spouses to be generous toward one another with regard to sexual intercourse. This of course, does not imply "sex on demand." Paul's challenge is for us to embrace a deeper attitude of generosity. This attitude refocuses our attention and sexual energy from our own gratification as our top priority toward focusing on our spouse's experience of pleasure as our number one concern. As our attention shifts from "What's in it for me?" toward "How can I give?" married sexual intercourse becomes a generous, rather than selfish, act.

Intimacy

Sex, in its deepest sense, is a reflection of the intimacy shared between a husband and a wife. In their book *Radical Hospitality*, Lonni Collins Pratt and Father Daniel Homan, O.S.B. offer great insight into the relationship between sex and intimacy. To that end I will quote them at length:

> Equating sex with intimacy contributes to our misunderstanding the true nature of intimacy…. Sex does not automatically create intimacy, as millions of people have painfully discovered. In making sex and intimacy one and the same, intimacy has been belittled while an entire set of faulty expectations of casual sex has been created. When we confuse intimacy with sexual relations, we imply that sex is the only means to closeness, and we devalue the growing together that two people need to do before they become sexually involved…. Intimacy, however, never crushes the human soul; it only builds up. Because intimacy regards the other as valuable and cherished, it makes us more human…. Intimacy is the deep experience of knowing another human heart…. Without intimacy, sex only deepens abiding and severe loneliness. The purpose of sex is to enhance an already intimate relationship; when we use it for any other purpose it fails us.[2]

In order for us to experience what God has intended for sex to be in our marriage, a couple must be diligent about working at being intimate outside of the bedroom. A woman I know likes to say, "Last night's sex began when he started doing the dishes."

Doctor Gary Smalley in his DVD *Hidden Keys to Loving Relationships*, suggests that in order for physical intimacy to be mutually fulfilling, a couple must attend to four levels of intercourse in a marriage.[3]

1. Mental intercourse. This involves connecting on a deep mental level. It is a desire and expression that you care and want to know more about your spouse's innermost thought processes.

2. Emotional intercourse. This is the sharing of our deep, inner feelings. Women tend to be more adept at this type of intercourse than are men, but men are capable of this level of sharing.

3. Physical intercourse. Meaningful touch, hugging, kissing, and caressing are all vital elements of physical intimacy. There is no set time when foreplay should begin. Attending to this type of physical intimacy is essential in order to enjoy gratifying sexual intimacy.

4. Spiritual intercourse. This is the highest form of intimacy shared by a couple. It occurs when you pray together, share and encourage morals, ideals, share religious experiences such as retreats, missions, and worship. It could be as simple as savoring together God's beauty and presence in nature.

Sex is not an isolated act in a marriage. When it is held in its proper place, it is woven within the very fabric of married life. When we focus on lovemaking, our attention shifts toward sex as a generous and loving act. This is what God intended—a beautiful gift and expression of love which in God's plan transmits grace and reveals God's love for the world.

Scripture: 1 Corinthians 7:3–5

The husband should give to his wife her conjugal rights, and likewise the wife to her husband. For the wife does not have authority over her own body, but the husband does; likewise the husband does not have authority over his own body, but the wife does. Do not deprive one another except perhaps by agreement for a set time, to devote yourselves to prayer, and then come together again, so that Satan may not tempt you because of your lack of self-control.

For Reflection

1. Which of the four levels of intercourse is strongest in your relationship? Which is lacking?
2. What practical things can each of you do to improve in the four levels of intimacy?
3. Each of you write out the following on separate pieces of paper in private and then come together to exchange and discuss:

    The thing I like most about my body is:

    The thing I like least about my body is:

    The thought of having sex with my future spouse or my spouse makes me feel:

6. How was sex portrayed in your home when you were growing up?
7. Did your parents talk with you about sex and sexuality? If so, what did they talk about?

CHAPTER FIVE

Money: The Real American Idol

Ken and Samantha met in college. After dating for several years they were both ready to get married. Only one thing stood in their way: During her college years Samantha had accrued thousands of dollars in credit card and student loan debt. And while for many couples, this is par for the course, this was simply unacceptable for Ken. It revealed a lack of discipline and self-control, and he was very concerned about how these bad habits would play out in their future marriage.

Ken was raised in a family that avoided debt at all costs and placed a high value on hard work, saving money, and financial security. Ken's father built the family business through years of hard work, sacrifice, and simple living. Ken did not fall far from the family tree. Ken remembers telling Samantha, "I love you very much and really want to spend the rest of my life with you. But I will not marry you until you pay off your debt. I'll help you. I mean I won't pay it for you, but I'll help you make a budget and encourage you to stick to it so that you can pay it off."

Samantha recalls that while at the time she was a little stunned, today she appreciates Ken's attention to their finances. "I know he is taking care of our family and will provide for our future. I've learned not to spend money in order to make me feel good. I think this helps our marriage a lot."

Debt Has Roots

In an episode of the TV sitcom *King of Queens,* Doug has an encounter with a salesman where they discuss some extra money he has become aware of:

> Salesman: So what are you going to do with the money?
> Doug: We're putting this money in the bank for our kids' college. Well, right after we get the hot tub and the satellite dish, but then, it's going straight to the bank.

Doug's response, while humorous, shows a real attitude of many people toward money. Everyone knows the importance of saving a portion of their income, but in reality the temptation to "buy now, save later" can be too great.

Lots of couples begin their new lives together with some amount of debt incurred before they met their spouse, such as in the case of Samantha. And while some couples are lucky to have their wedding and honeymoon paid for, many couples return from their honeymoon and face a hill of debt that requires their immediate attention.

This type of debt in and of itself is not deadly. Were that the only type of debt faced by couples, it could, as in the case of Samantha, be systematically paid off by following a reasonable budget.

More often couples find themselves buckling under the weight of a different type of debt—one that has roots in immediate gratification, impulsiveness, and impatience. This needs to be examined and discussed in order to avoid serious money problems down the road.

Money Has Power

Money's power comes in different forms. On one hand, it can be traded for goods or services. On the other, it has the power to reveal to us what we value most. If we value a healthy body and the way we look, then we're going to invest in exercise equipment or a gym membership. If we value food or cooking, then we'll invest time and money in the kind of cookware or ingredients we buy. If we value our appearance, we might buy a lot of cosmetics, hair, or skincare products. If we spend money and time doing things like socializing and going out to dinner, then we place a high value on entertaining. As I mentioned in the last chapter, show me your calendar and checkbook register, and I'll be able to tell you what you believe is important.

Money has power—inherent power. It doesn't need to do anything or be used for anything to have power. I could bring you into a room with a million dollars in cash stacked upon a table and I would be willing to bet your pulse rate and breathing would change. Just looking at all that money would do something to you. That is why our society for a long time has held taboos surrounding talking about money. Along with religion and politics, I have always understood not to talk about money in certain company. I know I am not alone.

Not talking about money has its advantages and disadvantages. In social settings it is probably good to not speak of the specifics of our financial situation. The taboo serves us well in this instance because it protects us from embarrassment and creates a sense of healthy boundaries among even the closest relationships. But it has some real drawbacks when entering into the sacrament of marriage.

Money gives us the ability to do things. It gives us the ability to acquire and gives us options. Because of this it gives us power. And in an intense relationship like that of marriage, an imbalance of power can lead to resentment. One technique of healthily discharging some of this power is to speak often and openly about the state of finances in one's marriage. There are many different ways to go about deciding who gets to spend how much on what and when, but before all of that comes, young couples will benefit from going into their engagement with an agreement and a shared value to speak often and openly about the state of their financial union.

Making a Budget

At the outset, it might be good to look closely at the connection between values and money. A good way to begin is to look at the many things you will have to spend money on when you are married:

Home (mortgage or rent)
Transportation
Utilities
Entertainment (this includes television and gaming)
Food (including eating out)
Education
Savings
Retirement
Children's college

These are just some of the major areas you will face when deciding where your hard-earned dollars will go. One of the most helpful exercises that Mindi and I did before getting married was to prioritize these things in order of importance to us. This helped us to see what one another thought was most important. And while it will feel good to gush about the areas you agree upon, it is far more worthwhile and productive to spend some time talking about the "hot spots" in which you differ.

Something that may help you get started is to acknowledge a common tendency toward perfectionism. Perfectionism is at the heart of an either/or mentality. We can tell that we are in perfectionist either/or mode whenever we find ourselves not doing something we know we should do. This is almost always at the heart of procrastination. In the back of our heads is a voice that says, "unless you can do this perfectly, why do it? Go spend your valuable time doing something you know you can do perfectly."

Give yourself permission to not have to have it all planned out just perfectly. And while there is a great deal of security and comfort that comes from a well-formed budget and financial plan, if having to have it all figured out is preventing you from even broaching the subject, then give yourself permission to not finish and to not do it perfectly. In addition to talking about the one subject that is at the root of most divorces, you will also receive some inner freedom over a common neurotic tendency toward perfectionism.

Joint or Separate Accounts?

One of the most fundamental decisions you will have to make about money is whether you will have joint or separate accounts. There are pros and cons to both. Mindi and I combined our accounts while we were engaged. We found that this gave us something healthy to do and talk about when we got together. It gave us practice communicating openly about spending and we got an early glimpse into one another's spending habits. We've kept joint accounts to this day. It has worked for us. Yet some couples have had the same experience with separate accounts.

Frank and Adele have been married for over thirty-four years and since their third month together they have used separate accounts.

"It's worked like a charm!" says Frank, with no small amount of pride. Now with direct deposit so common and so easy Frank and Adele have their monthly paychecks deposited to each of their accounts. They made decisions long ago who would pay what from their account. This evens out the disparity in their salaries and leaves them both with about the same amount after bills, and savings to spend as they wish, though there have been a few times when they've needed to ask one another for money in order to make a special purchase. This helps keep them accountable for what they spend.

With all the couples I've spoken with, there's no right or wrong way. Remember Ken and Samantha from the beginning of the chapter? Ken sent me this e-mail update on their financial situation:

> Samantha has become very good about spending money. I don't have to question anything she does with our money. I do all the investing and tell her where the money is. I trust her 100 percent and know she will always do the right thing even if I die. That is very important to me.
>
> After almost ten years of marriage we are still solving money problems. At least not big ones though I want to get this right so we can teach our kids the right way of doing it.

For those who enjoy working with money, handling it, and managing it, dealing with finances when married may come naturally. For most couples however, issues about money and surrounding money will call them to exercise great patience, discipline, and engage in frequent, open, honest communication.

Scripture: Matthew 6:19–21, 24

> Do not store up for yourselves treasures on earth, where moth and rust consume and where thieves break in and steal; but store up for yourselves treasures in heaven, where neither moth nor rust consumes and where thieves do not break in and steal. For where your treasure is, there your heart will be also.
>
> No one can serve two masters; for a slave will either hate the one and love the other, or be devoted to the one and despise the other. You cannot serve God and wealth.

For Reflection

1. What value do you place on financial security?
2. In what ways do your spending and your values match up? In what ways are they misaligned?
3. What values around money did you bring with you from your family of origin? Which of those serve you well? Which ones do you think you should let go?
4. Are you more comfortable with joint or separate accounts? Why? What do you see as the advantages and disadvantages to both? In what ways will one work better for you?
5. Do you have a budget? What might a sample budget look like for you at this time?
6. What beliefs do you have surrounding debt? Did you bring debt into your marriage? How are you working through it?

Married With Children—Openness to New Life

There they were. Two lines. Two pink lines that changed my life.

I can't remember how many times I asked Mindi to check and recheck the pregnancy test to make sure it was accurate. I insisted we take multiple tests, in order to rule out the 1-percent chance the test was wrong. Each positive sign or digital readout that said "pregnant" confirmed we were having a baby. Wow! I felt proud, afraid, excited, and insufficient at the same time and I hadn't even held my child yet. We'd only known we were pregnant for less than thirty seconds and yet something had changed. I was different. We were different. We were no longer just husband and wife, we were also Mommy and Daddy.

Nine months later I stood in the delivery room holding my son, Max. I was all smiles and felt "responsible." Never before had someone really needed me. In all of my life, all of my relationships, there was always a measure of dispensability. Even though Mindi and I grew to depend upon one another, we knew that if something happened to either of us we'd be fine. We were self-sufficient long before we were married. But now, in my arms was a magnificent, fragile baby who depended upon me for its most basic needs.

Mixed tears of pride and joy swelled in my eyes. Looking at

Mindi, I was humbled by her amazing courage during childbirth. Months of anxious anticipation, fluctuating hormones, mood swings, weight gain (both of us—sympathy eating is a real deal!), assembling baby furniture, and attending showers culminated in this extraordinary moment. It was awesome.

Two days later, operating on less than a total of seven hours of sleep, I was jumping out of bed panic-stricken and stumbling through our dark, cluttered foyer toward Max's crib. I arrived with mirror in hand, having learned that since you can't always hear a baby's breathing and worried that I'd swaddled him to death, condensation on a mirror held up to his nose would be a vital sign adequate to ease my mind.

During the first couple of weeks having Max at home, those feelings of pride, excitement, and awe were replaced by a persistent nagging performance anxiety, irritability, and utter exhaustion. With heightened states of arousal, we who could (and did) sleep through raging hurricanes, were now simultaneously jumping out of bed and sprinting into Max's room responding to imagined screams, only to find him sound asleep in his crib. It was a constant state of red alert.

This wasn't in the brochure! Our friends had given us plenty of advice and done their best to prepare us for having a baby, but what about this? At their recommendation I had within arm's reach the most sophisticated baby merchandise in the history of civilization, but not once was I warned about sleep deprivation, and its subsequent symptoms. "Was this some sadistic rite of parental passage?" I wondered.

Within four weeks, we along with Max were sleeping through the night. Things were much, much better, yet still very different. Not bad, but different. That little bundle of joy required a great deal of our attention and energy—two precious resources once exclusively available for our relationship, social life, and individual interests. While driving, our attention shifted from sporty SUVs to cavernous minivans that were capable of hauling an arsenal of baby equipment. Our pastime of people watching changed from noticing the latest trends in fashion to the latest and greatest in stroller design. We suddenly had more to talk about with friends who had children, and less with those who did not. Our lives, once carefree and not restricted by time, now revolved around Max's feeding and napping. Like I said: *a major adjustment.*

And while every couple prepares and adjusts differently below are some of the things that have worked well for many of the couples I interviewed for this book:

- *Find and read practical, helpful books, blogs, and articles.* There are lots of books on preparing for childbirth, making the transition and caring for a baby. The Internet is a great source of information. One thing Mindi found helpful was the reader comments from bookseller sites. We would base purchases on the types of reviews items received from other parents. Don't limit your reading preparation to books. There are many blogs and magazines out there for new and expecting parents.
- *Consider taking a parenting class.* Some find taking a class a useful and organized way of preparation. Many of these are free and they are extremely practical and helpful. Check with your hospital or obstetrician's office to see what's available in your area.
- *When the baby sleeps, you sleep.* Months of poor sleep, anticipation, anxiety, and nesting take its toll on you. Without enough sleep you'll be no good for your baby. Many couples call this the "golden rule" of the first few weeks and months. As much as possible, reduce extra activities to catch up on much-needed rest.
- *Ask for and accept help from family and friends.* Ask for help and

allow others to help you. Even more helpful than the meals friends and family provided were the nights they came over to let us sleep while they took care of feedings and diaper changes. People want to help, and they'll look to you in order to find out how. Ask for what you need and want. There will be plenty of opportunities to return the favor.

- *Make time for your marriage.* I'll never forget the words of a friend, "Before you were a dad, you were a husband." Before the baby, there was plenty of time to address issues that came up in the relationship, go on dates, hang out with friends. After the baby, you will need to intentionally squeeze in time for dates, marital communication, lovemaking, and alone time. What's best for your baby is what's best for your marriage. Remember marriages don't have a shelf life. They require constant attention—even with a new baby. As soon as you feel it's appropriate to have a trusted babysitter, get out of the house, go on a date, and talk about anything other than the baby.

- *Savor this beautiful time.* Nothing compares to holding your child. Take time to savor this moment. It will only happen one time with this child. Make the most of it.

- *Practice letting go.* Ten years from now no one will remember that your house was a wreck or the lawn looked unkempt. Trying to maintain normality while adjusting to life with a baby is unrealistic and futile. Something's going to give and it'll probably be your sanity. It's OK to leave some things undone.

- *Practice faithfulness, not perfection.* It is quite common, especially for mothers, to become overwhelmed with feelings of guilt and inadequacy. Take solace in knowing that nobody knows it all and nobody has ever done it perfectly. Be prepared to make mistakes and try to laugh them off. Babies are resilient little creatures. What they need most is love, care, and attention.

What Type of Parent Do You Want to Be?

While it's not practical to believe that you can visualize in great detail the skills and tools you will need (and feel comfortable using), you can begin to conceptualize a broad parenting philosophy. There are some things you feel strongly about, either for or against. Since no one is perfect, it makes sense that your parents were not perfect as well. Figuring out what things our parents did we would like to keep and which things we would like to let go are essential to forming our own parenting philosophy. It is healthy to discuss this because voiced or not they will unconsciously guide the way you raise our kids. Marital conflicts occur when there is a difference in philosophy that has not been discussed.

No matter how you envision yourself as a new parent, rest assured that "parenting" is not a genetically inherited personality trait. It is a set of learnable skills. Some people are more adept at picking up these skills than others, perhaps. Some have more exposure to effective parenting skills, but parenting can be learned.

Four Parenting Styles

Psychologist Dianna Baumrind spent years observing parents and children and has culled from her work four main styles of parenting:

- *Authoritative.* The authoritative parenting style attempts to direct child behavior in an active, rational way. It encourages dialogue while maintaining that the parent, not the child, is the authority figure. These parents value a child's autonomy and disciplined conformity to family rules and structures. Authoritative parents affirm their children's positive qualities but do not shy away from setting standards and realistic expectations for behavior.

- *Authoritarian.* This parenting style is like that of a dictator. There is little room for dialogue as obedience and submissiveness are heralded as the chief virtues of good children. It places little, if any value on autonomy and creative individual expression while maintaining absolute, unbending standards for behavior.

- *Permissive.* The permissive parent holds a non-punishing, accepting, and affirming style in most situations, even when unwarranted. In a permissive home, the child is consulted and given a vote in family policies, and rules are always followed by detailed reasoning and explanation. This parent makes few demands on the child's behavior. Permissive parents do not require much in the way of individual responsibility. This parent sees himself as a resource, not as an agent helping the child to learn responsibility and self-control.

- *Uninvolved.* These parents also tend to make few demands upon their children. They also tend to be nonresponsive to both positive and negative behaviors. While these parents are not abusive, this style of parenting borders on neglectful. The children of uninvolved parents perform poorly in many areas of life.

Discipline

For some the word *discipline* conjures up negative images of spankings and harsh dictator-like treatment of children. The root meaning of the word *discipline* is "follow." When we discipline our children, we are helping them to follow a certain standard of being and behaving that is predetermined by parents. The following are a few tips regarding discipline:

- *Be firm rather than rigid or passive.* Ideally, firmness is a middle ground of rigidity and passivity. Neither one of those extremes in parenting style is good for children. Firmness allows one to be yielding when appropriate yet able to withstand child resistance.
- *Use logical rather than relational consequences.* Logical consequences are things like time out and removing a privilege or a toy for a certain period of time. Relational consequences are exercised in facial expressions, word choice, and tonality of voice which convey disappointment and a message of "because you did this behavior Mommy or Daddy doesn't like or love you as much." Now, few parents ever intend to communicate this message, but if we are not careful we do. A good rule of thumb here is to always practice good words, good facial expressions, and good tone of voice. This can be especially hard when we are frustrated, tired, or angry.
- *Be clear about expectations.* With children, especially younger children, clarity comes through repetition. You'll find yourself repeating your expectations a lot. That's OK—it's normal. As children grow older, clarity will come through extended dialogue about what is appropriate and what is not appropriate.
- *Assure understanding.* When a child is old enough, make sure they understand what it is you are asking of them. As mentioned in chapter two, communication is a complex process. Sometimes kids don't hear us say what we think we are saying. In most cases this type of confusion can be clarified by asking, "What is Mommy (or Daddy) asking you to do?"
- *Solicit consent.* This is where you get your child to "buy in" to the expectation and consequence. Once they understand what it is you are expecting of them, you might ask, "How does this sound?" to give your child an opportunity to indicate that he or

she has agreed to this expectation and its stated consequence.

• *Exercise swift enforcement of consequences.* Especially with younger children, the more quickly consequences are administered and enforced, the more effective they will be.

As with the other areas of parenting, this too is a learned skill. As you gather more information about discipline, through books, articles, blogs, and friends, you will integrate that into your own style of effective discipline. It will no doubt modulate over time, and that's to be expected. What's important is that discipline, like all aspects of parenting, is intentional rather than reactive.

Remaining Open

Ken always wanted a family, though there was never a particular number of kids in mind. Having their first child meant for Ken that he could to do a little less hunting, a little less fishing, and a few less things for himself, which was fine. By the time he and Samantha had their second child, Ken was convinced there would never be a third. He was famous for saying "I've got two—one boy and one girl. I'm through!" But Samantha felt differently. She did not have a goal for a specific number of kids, but she felt that they were not being "open" to life, as they had promised at their wedding. She never pressed the issue with Ken, but prayed for him to be more open. Ken recalls, "At that time I wasn't interested in what God wanted for my family. It was what I wanted, or didn't want—and that was another child."

One evening a group of close friends challenged Ken about his closed-mindedness. "It was like God was speaking to my heart," Ken recalled. In the following months Ken felt his heart softening and becoming more open to letting God into his family.

Today with four kids Ken says, "I am still open for more children if that is what God wants for our family. Every day when I walk into my living room and my kids run and jump into my arms and hug me—that's it. That is my joy. It is that joy which reminds me every day what life is about and what I am living for."

The point of this story is not "the more kids you have the happier you will be." Because that is not necessarily true. The lesson is that we will only find the fulfillment, significance, and happiness we long for in the degree to which we remain open to God's Spirit at work in our life. In marriage one of the ways we remain open to the Spirit is by being open to the gift of children. The Second Vatican Council's Pastoral Constitution on the Church in the Modern World states,

> Parents should regard as their proper mission the task of transmitting human life and educating those to whom it has been transmitted. They should realize that they are thereby cooperators with the love of God the Creator, and are, so to speak, the interpreters of that love.... Let them thoughtfully take into account both their own welfare and that of their children, those already born and those which the future may bring. For this accounting they need to reckon with both the material and the spiritual conditions of the times as well as of their state in life.[1]

The document goes on to say that in making their decision parents should seek to inform their conscience, while discerning how they can be most open to God's spirit and the gift of new life.

This requires prayerful and thoughtful consideration. What does it mean to be open? For some, it means having children right away while for others waiting for a while is what's most prudent. There is no magical time frame that works for every couple.

One tendency to be mindful of during this discernment process is drifting to extremes. On one side is blind disregard for the practicalities of life. On the other is total rejection of children altogether. God calls us to the middle. Openness asks that we consider the practical circumstances of our life—like bringing children into the world. It means that we bring our desires and fears before God and ask for grace. It means that we are honest with ourselves about our true reasons for not wanting children if that is indeed the case. It doesn't ask that we commit to having x-number of children, but rather that we commit to honestly evaluating all of our resources, financial, emotional, spiritual, and relational. After making all of these careful considerations, God asks that we respond with a spirit of generosity by growing our family in accord with the Spirit.

Natural Family Planning (NFP)

Natural Family Planning is a natural method for couples to space out children based on a woman's menstrual cycle. The couple does this by monitoring the woman's body temperature throughout the month and noting thermal shifts which indicate times of fertility and infertility. When a couple has discerned that it is not a good time for them to have children, they can choose to have sex during the time of the month when the woman is infertile.

Although my wife and I have studied and practiced Natural Family Planning since the beginning of our marriage, I remain no expert at it. For more in-depth information, I would recommend you visit the Web site of the Couple to Couple League— www.ccli.org. It has a host of resources available about NFP.

Scripture: Proverbs 22:6

Train children in the right way,
and when old, they will not stray.

For Reflection

1. How many children would you ideally like to have? Are you "open" to children?
2. Have you considered practicing Natural Family Planning (NFP)?
3. What was the parenting style of your parents? What techniques will you adopt from them? Which will you change? Why? How?
4. What type of parent do you want to be? What do you want your children to say about you after you are gone?
5. How might your relationship change with the addition of children? How has it changed? What has remained the same?
6. Which of the tips presented seem doable or workable in your life?

CHAPTER SEVEN

CSI: Marriage: Who's Right? Who's Wrong?

Rachel and Scott were high school sweethearts. After three wonderful years of marriage they, like many couples, wanted a baby. That process wasn't easy. They struggled for over a year to get pregnant. Month after month they would go on that emotional rollercoaster of anticipation and disappointment.

Watching their friends get pregnant and have children was difficult and they did their best to disguise their jealousy and be happy for them. After one miscarriage their time had come. They were elated. What a relief. After almost a year of intentionally trying to get pregnant, trying everything from boxer shorts to vitamin E samples, they had conceived their first child and were in the "safe zone" (not likely to have a miscarriage) at the end of the first trimester.

In the middle of the second trimester their doctor told them that the ultrasound indicated that their baby had a rare heart defect and if the baby made it to term, he would most likely need immediate postnatal surgery. The doctors warned that complications were likely and could be serious.

Rachel and the baby made it to term and as expected baby Cooper was rushed into surgery just hours after delivery. Over a period of two and a half months Scott and Rachel lived away from home, near the hospital so they could be there every day with Cooper. After two surgeries and two and a half months of being covered in tubes, Baby Cooper went home to God. The physical, emotional, and spiritual strain endured by Scott and Rachel and their family and friends was enormous. At the final tally their portion of the medical debt after the insurance had paid towered near the $4 million mark.

This would be enough to wreck the best of marriages. The overwhelming burden of pregnancy complications, and a hospital ordeal that lasted months was exhausting and strained their relationship.

In the months following Cooper's death, Rachel and Scott grew distant. Rachel was slipping into a noticeable depression, having frequent suicidal thoughts, unexpected crying spells, and a deep lingering sadness. Scott, not knowing how to handle Rachel's problems and feeling powerless to help her, withdrew to the garage working on projects in an attempt to keep his mind off of the loss of Cooper and now what seemed to be a loss of his once vibrant, happy-go-lucky wife.

Their boiling point came one day when Rachel, in an attempt to reach out to Scott, asked, "Will you still love me if I'm (depressed) like this for the rest of my life?" Scott responded as truthfully as he could in the moment, "I don't know." It wasn't long after that that they came in for counseling. In only one session Rachel was able to see how her question to Scott was loaded and unfair, and Scott was able to see that what Rachel was really saying was, "I don't understand what's happening to me. I cannot fix it and I need to know that you still love me."

While Rachel and Scott's situation is unique, the issue that brought them to counseling is quite common. Conflicts occur in every relationship, even in the best of relationships. What distinguishes lasting relationships from those that don't make it is the ability to recognize potential sources of conflict, acknowledge when conflict is happening, and work constructively through toward resolution. It sounds simple, but in reality, there is probably no other facet of married life more difficult.

When conflicts arise, our natural inclination is to slip into whodunit mode and believe that if we can just find someone to blame, someone to pin the crime on, things will be better. The ancient Jewish people believed this to such an extent that they gathered once every year on the Day of Atonement to lay their sins on an innocent goat. They would literally lay the blame and sin of an entire nation upon an animal and send it off into the wild. And as tempting as it might be to think that we've progressed as a culture from such ancient modalities, the popularity of shows like *CSI* and countless others that mesmerize us with mysterious plots, promising to find the one responsible and bring them to justice, prove otherwise.

It's a popular model because it's easy to assign blame. It's much simpler to blame someone than to accept mutual responsibility if necessary and work together toward a peaceful solution.

The main problem with the scapegoat model of conflict resolution is that it is based on a false assumption that once we figure out who's wrong and get them to admit it, the problem is over. That's overly simplistic. It doesn't account for deeply entrenched needs to be right and a natural human need to save face.

Fighting Fair
In Sue Monk Kidd's popular book-turned–major motion picture, *The Secret Life of Bees*, the main character, August, a successful bee

keeper, offers advice about what she calls "bee yard etiquette" that I think is just as applicable to marriage. She says,

> [T]he world was really one big bee yard, and the same rules worked fine in both places: Don't be afraid, as no life-loving bee wants to sting you. Still, don't be an idiot; wear long sleeves and long pants. Don't swat. Don't even think about swatting. If you feel angry, whistle. Anger agitates, while whistling melts a bee's temper. Act like you know what you're doing, even if you don't. Above all, send the bees love. Every little thing wants to be loved.[1]

It's easy to forget the love we have for our spouse when tensions get high. Spouses would do well to practice "bee yard etiquette" when they are in the midst of marital conflict: Be gentle, speak softly, and don't swat, physically or verbally.

When people say that words don't hurt, they are lying or they just may not have heard the words that hurt them yet. Words do hurt, because they are our primary vehicle for communicating feelings and thoughts. When tempers flare and emotions are supercharged, as they can get in an argument or disagreement, process these in a way that is productive and not blaming—one that deescalates tension rather than pours more gas on the fire. Some suggestions for doing this are:

- *Be solution minded.* We are creatures who love blame. Blaming only serves to satisfy our need to be right; it does little to resolve conflict.
- *Avoid generalizing.* When we are in the middle of an argument or disagreement it's as if generalizations just seem to roll off of our tongues. Whenever we hear ourselves begin to say, "You always _____" or "You never _____," we are about to make

a generalization. We can also generalize by failing to qualify claims. For example, "You are an inconsiderate person." It's probably more accurate to say, "When you don't lower the toilet seat, I feel that you aren't considering my wishes."

- *Listen actively.* This means making and keeping eye contact, not interrupting, asking follow-up or clarifying questions, and focusing on what the other is saying rather than formulating our response. (Refer back to chapter two for greater detail on listening skills).

- *Communicate understanding.* Reflecting back to the other person what we heard them saying and asking, "Am I hearing you correctly?" is a powerful tool in effective communication. Other questions such as, "Is there anything else you need to say before I respond?" and finally, "Do you feel heard (understood)?" gives our spouse the opportunity to acknowledge that we're listening and that we understand his or her point.

- *Leave the past in the past.* Bringing up old wounds, past hurts, or disagreements only serves to widen the crevasse between spouses. A good rule of thumb is that what is in the past is out of play. Focus on the problem at hand, the current situation, current behaviors that are unacceptable. Use current examples. Resist the temptation to generalize character flaws by dredging up old material from the past. When we're reaching into the past for more evidence to bolster our argument, there's a good chance we're operating out of our need to be right, instead of a deep desire for peaceful resolution.

- *Attack the problem, not the person.* Attacking the person is the weakest form of argument that exists. But it's the easiest, and most effective at getting a response, so it is used a lot. You hear it when small children argue. Johnny confronts Luke about stealing his toy and Luke responds, "Oh yeah? Well, you stink!" That may be true, but that is not the issue. Making personal attacks or remarks in an argument only escalates it.

- *If possible, hold hands.* Holding hands while arguing helps to remain focused on the issue. It makes it hard to be mean to someone when you are holding his or her hand.

- *Find a good time to fight.* I've learned that discussing important or sensitive topics right before bedtime is not a good idea. We're both exhausted from a long day and wanting more than anything to get to sleep. We're not patient nor do we have the energy to listen well. And like most people, we're most prone to irritation when we're tired. We've found that the mornings, even if we have to wake up earlier, and weekends are the best times for us. This might include making sure you have eaten, and more importantly that you are not drinking alcohol.

- *Establish and respect a "time out" rule.* Many verbally inclined people like to argue. We see every disagreement or issue as a nail and words as our hammer. The problem is that disagreements come in all forms, not just nails, and sometimes we need to lay aside the hammer. It's taken me seven years to learn to be patient and give Mindi a lot of rope when we are arguing or discussing sensitive topics. Give your spouse permission to call a time out so that they can mentally and emotionally regroup. This prevents things being said that should never have been said.

- *Refuse to throw in the towel.* It's OK to take a break and call a truce, when we intend to return to the issue. If we walk away or throw in the towel with little or no resolution, we may be leaving behind hurt feelings and misunderstandings, not to mention an unresolved issue.

- *Be kind.* This doesn't mean we have to always be nice, but God does ask us to be kind to one another. This means that we refuse to engage in name-calling or make insulting, disrespectful, or demeaning remarks to our spouse. It means that we also respect each other's "hot spots," and refuse to take cheap shots at one another. My advice to couples in marriage counseling is: "Be kind to one another. No cursing. No name-calling."

The television host and popular American psychologist Doctor Phil McGraw is famous for saying: "Would you rather be right or happy?" This question that he poses to many guests on his regular show highlights the importance of having conflict resolution skills.

Mindi and I have thoroughly enjoyed being married. There have, however, been some rough patches over the years. There have been issues we have disagreed over and values which have surfaced that have cast us both over into the "dark side." Without a thorough commitment to see each of these issues through, using prudence and whatever charity we could muster up, we would not have made it this far.

Marriage is wonderful and within it we have unprecedented opportunities to experience God's grace and fulfillment. But like all good things worth having, it requires some work. Part of this work is learning and practicing the skills of conflict management and resolution.

Trip Wires

Soldiers in the military are trained to look out for hidden wires that when triggered, set off explosives. These wires have been carefully camouflaged so that the unsuspecting will inadvertently trip over them and set off an explosion.

Every person has their own set of emotional trip wires. These are those deep wounds, hurts, and beliefs that when aroused, conflicted, or otherwise tripped provoke within us intense reactions. They may be hidden so deeply that we either forgot they were there or we never knew they existed in the first place. Often it is not until our spouse or someone else trips and sets them off that we become aware of their presence—and power.

Mindi and I assigned several important household roles before we got married. I hated laundry and she hated the kitchen—all of it. Cha-ching! This worked well until one evening when I was swamped with take home work, and thus unable to clean the kitchen, I wondered aloud, "Why can't she just once clean the kitchen and load the dishwasher for me." Kaboom!

I had stepped over a trip wire. Once the shrapnel landed and the smoke cleared, Mindi shared that being in the kitchen was not fun and brought back unpleasant memories, whereas for me, it was fun and reminded me of some of our best family gatherings, cooking, laughing, and even cleaning while listening to music. This, albeit a fairly minor issue, when explored in a healthy, gentle way gave me a better understanding of her disdain for being in the kitchen. Furthermore, I was comforted by realizing that her reluctance to help me was not laziness or a lack of love for me, but a reaction to an issue from her childhood.

As counterintuitive as this may sound, sometimes having our trip wires set off can be beneficial. It can be an opportunity for us to recognize the connection between what life throws at us and our reaction to it. When we risk exploring what's really going on beneath the surface, what's provoking those intense feelings and reactions, and are able to process them internally or with another person, we can grow as individuals and as a couple.

Some trip wires are more serious than others. We may inadvertently stumble over major issues such as abuse, abandonment, or other painful wounds from our past that hold the power to instill acute emotional pain when triggered. Sudden withdrawal, intense anger or sadness can be a good indicator that we've stumbled upon an especially sensitive issue. Many relational blowups can be prevented by simply being mindful of the possibility that there may be other psychological and emotional factors at work in any given situation. If you suspect that there is something dwelling deeper beneath the surface it's OK to ask, "Is there something going on here that I'm not seeing?" As you proceed, keep in mind the following:

- *Be gentle.* Because you may not know the severity of the issue you're dealing with, it's always a good idea to be gentle. In the way you'd offer gentle care for a physical wound, you should do the same for emotional wounds.

- *Assume their best intentions.* Too often we assume that when our spouse does something that aggravates or offends us it is intentional, when it is usually something of which they are not even aware. Practice giving one another the benefit of the doubt. It takes time to gain insight into our patterns of behavior and it is essential that spouses give one another the time, space, and freedom necessary for self discovery.

- *Seek to empathize.* Know that we all have our own trip wires. When you find yourself reacting negatively to your spouse's, try to remember a time when you were in a similar position.

- *Offer compassion.* This can happen with words, or just a simple touch. Refer to the section on love languages to see how your spouse would prefer you to show love.

- *Be patient.* Awareness or insight does not necessarily produce change right away. Healing and growth happen over time.
- *Offer space.* Give them physical and emotional space to sort through what just happened. For serious wounds people need time to recover from the flood of emotions, much less begin piecing together the scene of the accident.

Compromise

One of the best things my wife and I did during our first two years of marriage was to begin openly discussing the importance of various issues as they came up and being open and honest about which ones were our hot buttons and which ones we could lay off. In his book *Tuesdays With Morrie,* Mitch Albom writes about a discussion he had with Morrie about the importance of respect in marriage:

> "I've learned this about marriage," [Morrie] said now. "You get tested. You find out who you are, who the other person is, and how you accommodate or don't."
>
> Is there some kind of rule to know if a marriage is going to work?
>
> Morrie smiled. "Things are not that simple, Mitch."
>
> I know.
>
> "Still," he said, "there are a few rules I know to be true about love and marriage: If you don't respect the other person, you're gonna have a lot of trouble. If you don't know how to compromise, you're gonna have a lot of trouble. If you can't talk openly about what goes on between you, you're gonna have a lot of trouble. And if you don't have a common set of values in life, you're gonna have a lot of trouble. Your values must be alike.

"And the biggest one of those values, Mitch?"

Yes?

"Your belief in the *importance* of your marriage."[2]

During the course of marriage preparation and the first years of a marriage, you will inevitably start noticing which issues are more important to you than others. Which are those that you cannot see yourself compromising on and which are the ones on which you believe you can compromise? The ability to compromise is an essential skill for any relationship. We cannot *always* have our way, even if we desperately believe that our way is the *right* way. We may have to decide at some point, "Would I rather be right, or would I rather be happy?" There can be many reasons a person has for needing to be right. Regardless, if you find that you are uncompromising on every issue, being in relationship will be difficult. Relationships work in the natural rhythms of give and take—a mutual exchange.

Another powerful skill that is practiced in lasting, healthy relationships is forgiveness. Rabbi Harold Kushner writes,

> ...two people with complementary personalities don't always fit together as neatly as pieces of a jigsaw puzzle. Sometimes there are mismatched edges that have to be worn down with love and patience. And that is why forgiveness, the readiness to accept traits in our partner that would drive us crazy if we didn't love them, and to accept them without a sense of martyrdom, sacrifice, or keeping score ("I put up with your snoring; how dare you criticize me for messing up the checkbook?") is the essence of married love.[3]

Forgiveness is a part of every loving relationship. It is impossible to truly love someone and not be able to forgive them. Our faith teaches us that we are to forgive others as God has forgiven us. In no relationship is this more important than in marriage.

Scripture: Ephesians 4:1–6

I therefore, the prisoner in the Lord, beg you to lead a life worthy of the calling to which you have been called, with all humility and gentleness, with patience, bearing with one another in love, making every effort to maintain the unity of the Spirit in the bond of peace. There is one body and one Spirit, just as you were called to the one hope of your calling, one Lord, one faith, one baptism, one God and Father of all, who is above all and through all and in all.

For Reflection

1. What were the unspoken rules surrounding conflict in your home growing up? What attitudes have you adopted regarding conflict? Is it acceptable? To be avoided at all costs? Does it ever work out?
2. How do you handle conflict today? What rules have you discussed about conflict in your marriage?
3. What things tend to push your buttons?
4. When is it most difficult to "fight fair"?
5. Is it OK to disagree with your spouse?
6. On average, how deep is your desire to be right? When was a time you were able to let go of being right, and found happiness on the other side? When has your need to be right not served you well?
7. What are the best times to have difficult conversations with your spouse? When are the worst? What are your "dead zones"?

Serenity Now! Nothing Can Make You Lose It Like Your In-Laws

Early in our marriage Mindi got frustrated with me, when after cutting and trimming the lawn I would come inside, covered in grass, spreading grass and dirt everywhere in the clean house. That was a problem. The solution? Since our yard was surrounded by a tall privacy fence, and there was a door to our bedroom in the backyard, it made sense that I should take off all of my clothes on our back patio before coming into the house. I could leave my clothes outside for Mindi to shake off and pick up later. That sounded great, and it worked just fine for almost two years until one hot Southern Louisiana summer day, when just after disrobing I went to slide open our backdoor and it didn't open. It was locked.

Naturally, I knocked on the door for Mindi to come let me in. After a couple of minutes she had not come. So I banged harder. What happens next is burned into my mind like a cattle brand. The curtains swung open and instead of my darling bride coming to my aid, there stood my mother-in-law. I don't know who screamed louder: she or I. Imagine a 300-pound man attempting to cover himself with a weed-wacker. Not a pretty sight. At family gatherings my mother-in-law loves to tell this story, always ending with:

"I wanted to get to know my son-in-law, but not *that* well!" Hardy, har har. Very funny. Pass the giblet gravy.

In one of the many classic episodes of *Seinfeld*, George's father, Frank, is having a problem with stress. His doctor advises him every time he faces a stressful situation to say aloud "Serenity now." Instead of saying it aloud quietly though, Frank throws his arms up in the air, regardless of where he is, and screams "Serenity now!" There are times when that's exactly what I want to do when dealing with both my and Mindi's family.

In my experience it's best to remember this when it comes to your in-laws: Although you rarely think of them, they are always thinking about you. My mother-in-law is always cutting things out of the newspaper for my wife, saving leftover plastic utensils from restaurants and there's never a weather change that we don't know about.

I honestly love my mother-in-law. And I'm not saying that because she'll be reading this book. She is always very proud of Mindi and me and I agree that she gives us plenty of space to live our own lives. When done in moderation, however, it can feel warm and protective and nurturing. She's not around too much, but she is always willing to be around when we need her, as in the case of needing a babysitter or a welcome bit of company in sharing a meal. I cherish the time my sons get to spend with their "Maw Maw."

I do know that my experience is not common for many couples. And perhaps there's no better person that fits the stereotypical "difficult mother-in-law" than Marie Barone, in the show *Everybody Loves Raymond*. Her meddling not only drives her daughter-in-law crazy, but it drives her son Ray crazy as well. Ray, still hamstrung by his controlling mother finds himself torn between obeying his mother and pleasing his wife. He often kowtows to his mother's wishes, which are frequently laden with manipulative guilt, and as a result always lands smack-dab in the middle of an argument with his wife.

And if it wasn't enough to sift through the expectations of your spouse, attempting to comprehend and meet the expectations of your in-laws or your parents when married can be trying.

One of the things about in-laws that is important to understand is that they are your spouse's parents. And most of us, when it comes to our parents, much like our children, don't tend to think logically or soundly. When it comes to our parents there is a lot of energy there that may not have been admitted, revealed, or expressed—some positive and some negative. Our family of origin has the ability to exert great influence on us because of the role they played in our early years. For good or ill, they helped shape who we are, and most of us, whether we like it or not, or will admit it or not, can be strongly affected by the actions or inaction of the members of our family.

But sometimes the situation will arise when for some reason or other we don't like our spouse's parents—perhaps it's because they are too involved, maybe they don't like us, and it might even be because they are too pushy and want to control our lives. And for many it's the exact opposite, they don't want to be involved enough.

Couples should discuss the involvement of their parents. In preparing for marriage it might be helpful to ask, "How much involvement are they going to have in our marriage? How much influence on our lives are we going to allow them to have?" Some couples find that sitting down with parents before the wedding or shortly thereafter in order to establish ground rules is productive, and saves them lots of resentment and conflict down the road. It might even be a good idea to sit down with both sets of parents ahead of time just to ask them what expectations they have of you.

Is It a Life Boat or the Titanic? *Getting Help From the In-laws*

Mike and Beth had decided early in their marriage that he would work and that she would stay home with the children. Mike earned an average salary, but it was work that he believed in. Beth supported Mike's calling to this ministry. Early on, accepting help from Beth's parents seemed like a win-win. What started with a down payment on a home over the years gradually extended to major home repairs and now private school tuition. Still, it was worth it. They lived a simple life. The money was used for important things, not luxury.

Mike noticed that while he appreciated the help and knew they couldn't afford their moderate standard of living without it, it was becoming increasingly clear that the checks were tied to strings of expectations. Beth's parents seemed to expect more say-so in how the kids were raised, the scheduling of time with the grandchildren during holidays, and other financial expenditures Mike and Beth made. Last, but not least, Beth's mom was calling or coming over every day unannounced.

After fifteen years of marriage and four children, Mike has a better, higher-paying job and while things still aren't perfect, they're much better. "I would say that you have to decide if you need the help or not, and then if you can either deal with any possible expectations or set firm boundaries. The spouse whose parents are offering the help must be the one to set the boundaries." Often this means looking closely at limiting family scripts.

Limiting Scripts

In the animated motion picture *Ratatouille*, Remy, a rat, longs to function as a chef among humans. His father thinks that is ludicrous, and constantly reminds Remy that he is a rat, and that trying to be anything else is futile and even deadly. Nevertheless, Remy moves forward and tries not to be dissuaded by his father's pessimistic script for him.

Nothing can pull on us like our parents and other members of our family of origin. Because of the influential role they played in our formative years and our level of dependence upon them, they hold an incredible power to influence us—even after we have grown up. As in the case of Remy, this can be detrimental to our growth as a person, and pull us backward.

We must learn to recognize when we are being pulled back into old scripts and roles. When we do become aware of this dynamic, we have an opportunity to set boundaries and remind our parents who we have become.

Here are some tips for establishing boundaries with your in-laws:

- *Use clear language.* Before attempting to set boundaries with your in-laws you must first be clear about what those are. This involves using clear and specific language. For instance, "I don't like how your mom comes over while I'm watching football on Sundays" is vague. It's a statement, but it's not clear. Instead, try: "Honey, would it be OK if we asked your parents to call before they come over and explain to them that Sunday is a day of recharging for me and I don't like to visit?" Crystal. Not only is that clear but it is accompanied by an effective, respectful request. Don't assume that you are both in agreement on something unless you've explicitly talked about it.

- *Present a united front.* Your parents should see you as a united front. This serves several purposes. First, it prevents triangulation. It's easy for a spouse and a parent to form an alliance against the other spouse. If all your mom or dad hears about is what your husband does wrong, they'll begin to dislike him. In all likelihood, they'll never know when you make up. Secondly, it presents a more powerful message and increases your chance at being effective. It also prevents you as an individual from shouldering the blame, should any finger-pointing take place.

- *Set and enforce boundaries.* Asking your parents to call before they come over and visit will serve no purpose, if you don't remind them of the boundary the first time they violate it. Not enforcing boundaries reinforces undesirable behaviors, and leads to a build up of resentment. Sometimes it may not be feasible to ask them to leave the moment they arrive unexpected, nor to discuss the matter during that visit. But it is crucial to have the phone call or visit the next day, in order to call attention to the boundary violation and reassert your request for respect of the boundaries you and your spouse have established.

- *If they are your parents, they are your responsibility.* If you are frustrated by the fact that your mom insists on vacuuming every time she comes over, it is not a good idea to ask your wife to confront her about it. She's *your* mother. And while there may be issues there and confronting them strikes a fear in you much like the day you brought home that bad report card in sixth grade, it's your responsibility to deal with your parents. Statements such as, "You talk to them please, they're not your parents," while understandable, reflect an immaturity and lack of taking responsibility.

- *Be supportive of one another.* Dealing with parents is tough work. Our families of origin hold a lot of influence in our lives no matter how old we are. Try to understand where your spouse is coming from and be supportive in their efforts to relate with their parents. This doesn't mean always turning a blind eye, but it does mean to avoid criticism. Criticizing is the most ineffective means of getting your way anyway.

- *"Honor your father and mother" does not equal being a doormat.* As a child the Sisters of Mercy drilled into my head the fourth commandment: Honor your father and mother. Honoring and respecting our parents does not mean that we allow them to make unreasonable demands upon us. We can respectfully acknowledge their expectations and reiterate to them what we have discerned is healthy for our own family.

Scripture: Exodus 20:12

Honor your father and your mother, so that your days may be long in the land that the LORD your God is giving you.

For Reflection

1. What expectations do your in-laws have of the amount of time you will spend with them?
2. Where will you spend the holidays?
3. What boundaries are you willing to put in place with your in-laws?
4. How much help are you willing to accept from in-laws? Physical, emotional, or financial? What strings *might* be attached to any assistance from your in-laws? Is it worth it?
5. How do you envision your in-laws being a source of support and encouragement?

From Sole Survivor to Soul Survivors:
Balancing an Individual and Couple Spirituality

"Please put your own oxygen mask on before helping children traveling with you." If you have ever flown on an airplane you have no doubt heard this pre-flight mantra. It's the airline's way of cautioning adult passengers against a natural inclination to take care of their children first. And while this sacrificial impulse is admirable, the airlines know that the best way to help children is for parents to first help themselves. Trying to put on a child's mask at the risk of your suffocation may end up killing both parent and child. What they know is that if you care for yourself first, the chances of you being able to care for both you and your child increase drastically.

The same is true in marriage. "Together forever" doesn't mean never leaving one another's side. A friend who has been married for over thirty years insists that one of the reasons for the success of his marriage has been to place a high value on taking time as individuals and as a couple away from the children, work, and the stress of everyday life. Once married, everything, including time and personal space, can seem like it's blending together, leaving some couples wondering where their own personal spirituality has gone.

When we do not reverence our individual selves by taking time to pray, rest, and recreate we soon run out of energy which is needed in order to maintain healthy relationships.

This doesn't mean that we constantly abandon our spouses and families for weekend retreats or spend hours on end reading religious and spiritual books. It does mean that we must find some method of feeding our own souls and find time for personal prayer.

I've learned that prayer, whether it is alone or as a couple doesn't just happen. It must be planned. As Doctor Robert Wicks states in his book *Living a Gentle Passionate Life,*

> If we merely feel that "our work is our prayer," reflect only when the feeling prompts us to do so or leave quiet reflection solely for unique, designated times during the day or week (Sunday?), we will then be left with an appropriately limited legacy; namely an artificial, narrow, undemanding relationship with our inner selves and with God.[1]

In addition to planning time for prayer, keeping it simple makes it easier to show up at those times. In this regard the A.T.R.I.P. method of prayer can be very helpful. A.T.R.I.P. is an acronym for Adoration, Thanksgiving, Repentance, Intentions, and Plan:

- *Adoration.* Begin by offering praise to God either aloud or in the silence of your heart. It may be helpful to select one of God's attributes, such as *merciful* or *loving* and praise God for that particular attribute.
- *Thanksgiving.* This is where you express gratitude to God for blessings and anything you might be thankful for.
- *Repentance.* We are all imperfect and broken, yet rarely do we risk sharing that with others. Acknowledging your brokenness

to your spouse does two things: First, it gives them permission to be broken, and second we feel loved and accepted despite our failures.

- *Intentions.* Mention all of the people and things you have promised to pray for. I've learned a lot about what's going on in the lives of our friends by listening to Mindi's prayer intentions. This also helps us to recognize what's important in each other's thoughts and prayers.

- *Plan.* Finally, come up with a plan for the next week or day, in light of the meditation or how God may have moved you during prayer or during the day.

You may want to close by holding hands and praying the Our Father, Glory Be, Hail Mary or a simple prayer of the heart and then offer each other the sign of peace.

In my experience, an essential element in beginning any spiritual discipline, whether it be as an individual or as a couple, is to *keep it simple.* If it gets too complicated or too involved, or too hard too soon, it can be tempting to rationalize not doing it. When it's simple and thought out your chances of actually praying together are much greater. Taking A.T.R.I.P. can last as long or short as you'd like, but we usually take about twenty minutes.

Some couples pray together by meeting for daily Mass once a week. Others have found making a designated holy hour together once a month or as often as possible to be very beneficial. Like all forms of prayer, how we pray is not as important as why we pray and *that* we pray.

When Your Spouse Seems to Lack Spirituality

Over the years as a minister and now as a counselor, I've listened to many spouses complain about their wives' or husbands' lack of spirituality. I always tried to help them see that it wasn't spirituality he or she was lacking; it was a connection between spirituality and what we commonly experience as worship. To some it might seem that certain people just aren't spiritual, or spiritually inclined. Nothing could be further from the truth. We all crave a spiritual connection. And while there is much, much more that can be said on this subject, I offer a few tips to help you effectively reach out to a spiritually distant spouse:

- *Be clear about what you want and what you are asking.* Vague generalities such as, "I want you to be more spiritual," or, "I just wish you had God in your life," are too vague and therefore easy to avoid answering. It is better to make clear, specific requests such as, "I would like you to join me at Mass every Sunday," or "I want you to exercise your spiritual leadership in this family by doing the following. . . ."
- *Believe in the importance of what you are asking.* If it's just something you "kind of" want or "sort of" would like, you can expect a weak response. Being passionate about wanting your spouse to get his/her spiritual act together is not guaranteed to work, but it will increase your chances of being effective—and it will also communicate that you are serious.
- *Be aware of the context in which you are asking.* If spirituality wasn't an issue while you were dating and engaged, and it is now a new priority (i.e., because of children) expect that your spouse may be surprised by your request and may require some time to adjust. And while setting a good example for your children is a great reason to ask him or her to "kick it up a notch," in his or her mind, this is news and he or she will need you to be patient.

However, if this is old news and it is something you discussed and agreed upon before marriage, then base your argument on holding your partner to the established agreement.

- *Seek help.* Suggest seeking spiritual advice. Allow your spouse to pick the individual you see, and talk about the main issues or concerns you have before going so that your spouse doesn't feel ambushed by you and the pastor or counselor.
- *Seek understanding.* Many of my female friends have shared with me that they have gained much insight about their husbands' spiritual journeys from reading books such as *The Wild Man's Journey* and *Adam's Return* by Richard Rohr and *Wild at Heart* by John Eldredge. For women the *Called to Holiness* series by St. Anthony Messenger Press offers a variety of insights into the unique struggles women face with their own spiritual growth. If possible, read the books together and discuss for mutual insights.
- *Pray for your spouse.* Saint Monica, Saint Augustine's mother, prayed for her son without ceasing. Ask God for the guidance, grace, and patience of Saint Monica, while your spouse struggles on his or her own faith journey.

Consider also that your husband or wife may be living out a script that was modeled for him or her. Be patient, and when possible lead by example, never force.

Creating Sabbath Time

The Jewish faith has passed on to us the beautiful restorative tradition of Sabbath rest, knowing that God designed his creation to be most fully alive when yielding to the ebb and flow of work and rest, work and play, work and pray. These are the natural rhythms of our life. Too often we think of the Sabbath as a day when we attend church, usually Sunday. Wayne Muller in his book *Sabbath* writes:

> Sabbath is more than the absence of work; it is not just a day off, when we catch up on television or errands. It is the presence of something that arises when we consecrate a period of time to listen to what is most deeply beautiful, nourishing, or true. It is time consecrated with our attention, our mindfulness, honoring those quiet forces of grace or spirit that sustain and heal us.[2]

Chet and Julie sensed that their lives had gotten too hectic and felt a need to slow down. They decided that the solution was to institute a "Sabbath" time in their home, a time when the TV would be off, only Christian songs would play on the radio, no video games would be played and no telephone calls would be made or taken unless it was an emergency. They did this from the time they woke up Sunday morning until they came back from Mass around noon that same day. They found that it enabled them to be more available for one another, have quiet time for family prayer, and enjoy some quiet time alone for prayer, hobbies, or simply relaxing. "God has definitely blessed our efforts in setting aside this time," Julie said not long after they began. "It just gave us all an excuse to *slow down*."

Chet and Julie's family Sabbath time is one way of creating a sacred space for God in their family. No doubt yours will be different. Remember that simplicity and fidelity are most important in the beginning. Working hard all week and keeping a busy schedule and shutting everything down on Sunday all at once is like trying to slam the brakes on a full-speed train. Of course, if Sabbath time is something you already practice and you are looking for ways to expand or deepen this practice, by all means take the next step.

Keep a Journal

Some find it helpful to use a prayer journal. If you decide to use a prayer journal, it can be as simple or complex as you want or need it to be. I know some couples who use their prayer journal as a way of reminding them of whom and what they have committed to pray for. This helps to remind us that there is a bigger world out there, and there are those with bigger problems than ours.

A couple's prayer journal may consist of each spouse taking a few moments before sharing to write down one or two sentences in each of the A.T.R.I.P. sections. (See the example that follows).

....

Reading

• Scripture passage _____

• Reflection _____

_____

_____

Adoration

What would I like to praise and adore God for today?

_____

_____

Thanksgiving

For what am I thankful for today? This week?

_____

_____

Repentance

What do I need forgiveness for? From whom? What areas of my life am I in need of grace and growth?

_____

_____

Intentions

Who has asked me to pray for them? What intentions would I like to offer to the Lord today? This week?

_____

_____

Plan

What is my plan for tomorrow, or next week? What things might I do differently? What might I stop doing? What can I start doing?

_____

_____

Moving Outward

Bill Wilson, the co-founder of Alcoholics Anonymous, was adamant that the only way a recovering alcoholic will remain sober is by finding and helping other alcoholics. It seems that Bill understood that after an initial period of sobriety, stagnation was not an option for the addict. If he or she didn't grow by reaching out and serving others, they would inevitably relapse and regress. This is the same underlying principle in evangelization. Jesus knew that we'd never be able to save the whole world, yet he calls his disciples to spread the good news. We can't just sit on the love we've been given to share. We've got to give it away! In the motion picture *The Bucket List,* a dying, but very wise, Carter Chambers (played by Morgan Freeman) reflected on what the ancient Egyptians believed about death. The Egyptians believed that when their souls got to the entrance to heaven, the guards asked two questions and the answers determined whether the dead were able to enter or not: Have you found joy in your life? Has your life brought joy to others?

In no way am I diminishing the wonder and importance of the honeymoon stage in marriage. That is an important and essential part of every marriage. There should come after a time of courtship, a celebratory experience of unity, of being together for the sole purpose of enjoying one another. But we should not stay there. Our souls, our egos cannot maintain such a prolonged state of celebration. If we are going to continue growing in happiness we must come down from the mountain top and get about some important work, some task, and some greater purpose.

Life asks us to change our posture from facing each other, to one of facing the world while hand in hand. It is a natural spiritual rhythm.

It can be difficult to maintain an individual spirituality in a sacramental relationship. In all of our efforts at communicating, blending, and focusing on our spouse, we risk losing sight of our own spiritual path which led us to marriage in the first place.

Scripture: Matthew 6:5–13

And whenever you pray, do not be like the hypocrites; for they love to stand and pray in the synagogues and at the street corners, so that they may be seen by others. Truly I tell you, they have received their reward. But whenever you pray, go into your room and shut the door and pray to your Father who is in secret; and your Father who sees in secret will reward you.

When you are praying, do not heap up empty phrases as the Gentiles do; for they think that they will be heard because of their many words. Do not be like them, for your Father knows what you need before you ask him.

Pray then in this way: Our Father in heaven,
hallowed be your name.
Your kingdom come.
Your will be done,
on earth as it is in heaven.
Give us this day our daily bread.
And forgive us our debts,
as we also have forgiven our debtors.
And do not bring us to the time of trial,
but rescue us from the evil one.

For Reflection

1. When was a time that you heard God in the sound of "sheer silence"?

2. Take out your readings from your wedding ceremony. How is God speaking to you through them today? How did he speak to you then?

3. What Scriptures or meditations do you find helpful in prayer?

4. What might a Sabbath ritual look like in your family or future family? What obstacles will you need to address and overcome?

5. Are you comfortable praying with your spouse? What challenges does couple spirituality present for you? How are you working through them? How have you asked your spouse to help you work through them?

6. Is grace before meals something that's doable in your marriage? If not, why not?

In Sickness and in Health, in Good Times and in Bad

About six years into our marriage I was forced to have surgery on my knee to repair a torn meniscus. The day after surgery I was feeling great, despite having only taken a small dose of my pain medicine. Three days later however, I was being rushed to the hospital to dissolve a blood clot in my swollen right leg. Upon hearing the news about the blood clot Mindi ran out of her work and rushed to the hospital to be with me. Upon examining my knee, the doctor informed me that my blood clot was the least of my worries. He was positive I had a serious infection in my surgical wound that needed immediate attention. He was right.

They rushed me into surgery to flush out the infection. That surgery didn't take. After another surgery and another round of intensive antibiotic treatments there was a ray of hope as the levels of infection seemed to decrease. I spent nearly two weeks in the hospital and was discharged and prescribed IV antibiotics for six weeks.

At home I slept only about thirty minutes at a time, if that. Thirty minutes is the amount of time it took the ice bag on my knee to melt. For over a month, every half hour, Mindi, having just fallen asleep herself, would get out of bed, change my ice bag, bring me medicine, and play along with (and often transcribe) my painkiller-induced hallucinations. To say she was patient would be a gross understatement. Not once during this whole ordeal did she complain about anything. Not once!

There were many moments when Mindi wished she could have taken my pain from me. I know there have been times when I wished the same thing for her. It's hard to watch anyone suffer—especially your spouse.

In the movie *The Lord of the Rings: The Return of the King*, Frodo Baggins and his buddy Samwise possess the ring and are bringing it to Mordor. At one point, the journey and the burden of the ring has overwhelmed them as they both lay on the mountain's side exhausted, delirious. Samwise, noticing Frodo's obvious exhaustion and the toll taken on him by bearing the burden of the ring says to him, "Come on, Mr. Frodo. I can't carry it for you. But I can carry you!"

That's exactly what Mindi did for me. She could not take from me my burden or even carry it for me. That was not her role. She did something much greater by lifting me up emotionally and spiritually during that difficult time.

I learned a great deal about myself during this time, and I learned even more about her. I learned just how much my wife loved me. I know this might sound bad, but I would have never imagined she was capable of such immense generosity and sacrifice when I married her. Sure, like all couples we promised to love each other in good times and bad, sickness and health, but in the back of my mind, I never believed that day would come. I certainly didn't think that vow would be tested six years later.

There's no expression that says "I love you" the way being with someone while they are ill, suffering, and depressed does. Mindi held me when I cried, even when it was obvious that it was a side effect of the pain medicine. She was constantly hopeful and optimistic on the days I was obsessing over whether I'd ever get better and make a full recovery. I know that somewhere and sometime without me knowing, Mindi had her meltdowns. The sheer load of raising a two-year-old and caring for her once jolly and energetic husband whose days had become a series of swallowing pain pills and watching cooking shows would take a toll on anyone. But she was strong throughout, never letting me see her struggle. During that time, she was entirely for me. I hope I can be that strong, that courageous, and that compassionate when, or if, my turn comes.

Coping With a Miscarriage

We were quite fortunate that Max was conceived without much aggressive planning and Mindi's pregnancy was without complication. Three years later as we tried to conceive our second child, we were not as fortunate.

After over a year of trying we finally conceived, only to have a miscarriage. It was heartbreaking. It's not an easy thing to go through. We weren't sure what to do and many of our friends and family felt the same way. Even in 2010, we lack as a culture any definitive set of norms to guide us in helping families grieve and cope with a miscarriage.

When a loved one who has been carried to term dies, we have in place religious and secular rituals and norms to guide us. People expect you to be sad. People expect you to grieve. There are expectations that you might/should take time off of work. People give you space to be where you are—not so much with miscarriages.

We didn't feel like talking about it, and at first we were aggravated with our friends for not reaching out to us. We didn't know if it was appropriate to have a religious service, and we were embarrassed to ask. We didn't want to look stupid or appear overly sentimental. Our hearts were broken, but our minds were not sure how to act. You hear that some people have several miscarriages before they decide to adopt or resign themselves to not having children. So you think, "Hey, even though I feel bad, this happens all the time and you never hear people talk about it so it mustn't be a big deal." Even when we were not thinking about it, our hearts were grieving a tremendous loss. Our wounded hearts needed healing. We turned to each other and to God. Eventually, we reached out to our friends and asked for what we needed: space, sympathy, and prayers. They were more than generous in every respect.

It is estimated that one out of every six recognized pregnancies will miscarry. There's no manual for couples telling them how to respond to this situation. I can only offer what worked for us.

- *Give yourself permission to be where you are.* There will be days when it seems as though the world is passing you by. It's OK to sit still. We often grieve and mourn in stillness. Know that there will be plenty of time to catch up with everything else later.
- *Ask for the help you need.* People don't know what they don't know. As much as we wanted folks to swoop in and help us through our situation, the truth is that most people just don't know how to handle a miscarriage. If there's no manual for you, neither then is there one for anyone else. Give friends and family an opportunity to meet your needs when you are able to identify what they are and ask for them.
- *Treat it as you would any other death.* Give yourself permission to grieve the loss of your baby just as you would any other death.

- *Have a ritual.* Mindi and I regret not having a ritual. Rituals can be powerful sources of healing and offer a sense of public (or semipublic) closure. It doesn't mean that grief is over by any means.
- *Take time off from work.* Most cultures accept taking time off from work as normal during a grieving period. It doesn't mean that you have to be alone, but it can give you space to process the early intense emotions. This does not necessarily need to happen right after your loss. Take the time when you need it.
- *Seek professional counseling if necessary.* Any time we lose a loved one it's difficult. The loss of a child is especially difficult. For some, professional or spiritual help during this time can be beneficial to the healing process.
- *Read books, online blogs, and other resources.* Tapping into blogs and other resources helps us to realize we are not alone. This can be very comforting when the world seems to be passing us by.
- *Don't blame yourself.* Most reasons for miscarriages are unable to be determined. Don't think that whatever it is you did caused this to happen. Our doctor was really comforting to us during this time. He explained that miscarriages happen for a myriad of reasons, and most of them have nothing to do with something the mother did or did not do.

Mental Illness

Upon finding out that they were pregnant with their first child, Katie and Richard decided that she would stay home with the baby for at least one year. She wasn't sure that she could do it emotionally. She found much joy and purpose in her work, and knew she would miss it. They knew that it would be financially difficult but concluded it was more than worth it.

Neither Katie nor Richard anticipated the hormonal changes that occur during pregnancy and childbirth. One afternoon when their son was six months old Richard got a phone call from Katie saying that she had reached her limit. That morning she had taken the baby to the local church and cried for what seemed like hours. She confessed that she was plagued with thoughts of bad things happening to Richard and their son.

They knew something was wrong but weren't sure what it was or what to do about it. A friend said that Katie might be suffering from depression and suggested seeing their doctor. Sure enough, the doctor agreed that Katie was indeed suffering from depression and prescribed antidepressant medication. The downside was that she would no longer be able to nurse her baby, something she really enjoyed. Richard was in shock that he hadn't realized what was going on with Katie. He prided himself on taking care of his family, but in the midst of working extra hours to compensate for the lack of Katie's income he somehow missed the symptoms of his wife's impending depression. "All the signs were there, right under my nose and I missed it," he recalls.

Katie was sick. But not in a way that we typically think of when we hear the word *sick*. Usually, we think of a disease, a cold, or some injury. Rarely, when we stand at the altar are we consciously promising fidelity to a person even when they suffer from mental illness. For a long time, mental illnesses were misunderstood and little information existed about them. As such there was, and still is to a certain degree, a stigma attached to them. We don't hesitate to tell someone that we've got the flu, but we tend to be very discreet about letting others know that we suffer from a mental illness.

Today we know a lot more about mental illness. According to the National Institute of Mental Health, one in every four Americans age eighteen and older suffers from a diagnosable mental illness in a given year. Nearly twenty-one million American adults suffer from a mood disorder such as depression, bipolar disorder, dysthymic disorder, anxiety and others, with the average age of onset being thirty years. Unlike common physical illnesses, mental illnesses are not always obvious and can be difficult to diagnose. There remain large sectors of our population that lack even a basic understanding of mental illness.

Prolonged Illness

Susan and Greg were young, hopeful, and enthusiastic about their future together as a married couple. Their love for each other could only be matched by their love of God and their faith. When they were married Greg was twenty-four and Susan was twenty-one. The world was at their feet. They weren't settled into careers yet, in fact they were both still in school working part-time jobs to support themselves.

Five months after their wedding Greg knew something was wrong. Susan, a once competitive athlete, was bumping into everything in the house and tripping over her own feet. Whereas she once steamrolled Greg on the tennis court, she was swiping at balls that were not even in the range of her racket. When she began waking up feeling nauseous and with terrible headaches, they went to a doctor who ordered an MRI. The results could have hardly seemed worse. There were tumors in several places around and on her brain. Her doctor was positive that she had developed Neurofibromatosis II, a rare genetic disease which affects one out of every 40,000 people.

Susan underwent several experimental surgeries seeking to improve her functioning and remove tumors that were pressing on her nerves. Because of the level of difficulty and specialization needed, they traveled a minimum of two hours and also journeyed across country to get the help she required.

Greg recalls, "I couldn't believe what was happening. It didn't seem real. I can't begin to describe the emptiness and abandonment I felt at the time. On drives home from the hospital, I would literally scream at God." Susan remembers thinking, "I don't want to spend the rest of my life like this. This is the lowest I've ever been. I'm not afraid of death, I'm afraid of life! It was a time of emotional and spiritual free fall. It was as though there was nothing to hold on to. The bottom had dropped out of our life and things were getting worse at an alarming rate."

Each specialist reinforced what they already knew: that each surgery, while offering a small glimmer of hope, also carried an extremely high risk of worsening Susan's condition and could even be fatal. Greg says, "I would often ask God, 'Why would you allow us to marry and then snatch everything away from us? How could you bless our union and then make it impossible to live out? What purpose could ruining our marriage possibly serve?'" He admits, "What I couldn't wrap mind my around at the time, and still struggle with today, in fact, was the possibility that maybe, just maybe, what we were actually doing *was* living out our marriage in exactly the way God wanted us to: true to our vows, self-sacrificially, and totally dependent upon him. Although I could not see it then, the success for our marriage we wanted so badly was coming in a way we did not foresee—by offering up our sacrifices to God."

Two years later, Susan still has an occasional surgery. She has regained most of her hearing but will likely spend the rest of her life dealing with spontaneously growing tumors throughout her body. Reflecting on what this ordeal means for them, Susan says, "I know it sounds cliché, but I make it a point to enjoy each day. You can never have it back when it's gone. If you spend your life waiting for the next 'thing' to happen, you'll miss the time that has passed. I don't take anything for granted anymore. This experience has only made me stronger. When you have to fight to live every day and hang onto hope for minimal quality of life, you really do get stronger. Ultimately, I'm learning to trust God with everything— my life, health, finances, marriage—everything."

To the same question, Greg says, "There once was a time when we were afraid of spiritual openness and vulnerability between each other. This has given us an opportunity to become less self-absorbed and more focused on our spousal love. I'm learning to accept that my ultimate concern must be holiness. Abandonment in God is the only way I can live. When this is my priority, current suffering and a certain future of suffering takes on a different perspective—from one of loss to opportunity, an opportunity to love Susan and God through service and sacrifice."

No one hopes to suffer. No one wants to suffer, much less watch their loved ones suffer. But suffering is a part of life. As Greg and Susan teach us, resistance is futile. It is only when we give ourselves over to it that we find within it meaning and purpose. When I consider the mystery of suffering and its relationship to my faith, I still struggle to make sense of it. A few years ago I came across an unpublished poem by Sister Carol Bielecki, R.S.J.C., entitled, "Breathing Under Water." I haven't read or heard anything regarding the Christian mystery of suffering since that speaks to my heart quite as powerfully.

I built my house by the sea.
Not on the sands, mind you;
not on the shifting sand.

And I built it of rock.
A strong house
by a strong sea.
And we got well acquainted, the sea and I.
Good neighbors.
Not that we spoke much.
We met in silences.
Respectful, keeping our distance,
but looking our thoughts across the fence of sand.
Always, the fence of sand our barrier,
always, the sand between.

And then one day,
—and I still don't know how it happened—
the sea came.
Without warning.

Without welcome, even
Not sudden and swift, but a shifting across the sand like wine,
less like the flow of water than the flow of blood.
Slow, but coming.
Slow, but flowing like an open wound.
And I thought of flight and I thought of drowning and I thought of
        death.
And while I thought the sea crept higher, till it reached my door.
And I knew, then, there was neither flight, nor death, nor drowning.
That when the sea comes calling, you stop being neighbors,
Well acquainted, friendly-at-a-distance neighbors,
And you give your house for a coral castle,
And you learn to breathe underwater.

I believe Sister Carol is right. Accepting God's presence, God's will in my life in both good times and bad, in sickness and in health, in life and in death has been a mysterious, fitful process, much like trying to breathe under water.

Scripture: Philippians 3:8–11

More than that, I regard everything as loss because of the surpassing value of knowing Christ Jesus my Lord. For his sake I have suffered the loss of all things, and I regard them as rubbish, in order that I may gain Christ and be found in him, not having a righteousness of my own that comes from the law, but one that comes through faith in Christ, the righteousness from God based on faith. I want to know Christ and the power of his resurrection and the sharing of his sufferings by becoming like him in his death, if somehow I may attain the resurrection from the dead.

For Reflection

1. Call to mind a time when a loved one was ill. What memories and feelings surface when you recall that event?
2. How do you respond to people when they are sick? Are you naturally compassionate? Do you tend to lack empathy? Are you one to take initiative or do you create distance?
3. How have you been the recipient of someone's compassion when you were sick? What is your response to suffering? How do you understand the nature of suffering in light of your faith? Your marriage vows?

Together Forever

The first five years of marriage should be the first of many years together.
A joy-filled life together is not only possible, but it is in fact what
God intended for marriage. There will be times of struggle, and
relationships do require work in order to bring us that sense of joy.
But it is good work—meaningful work.

No marriage is free from times of struggle. No vocation or state
in life is. Everyone will experience good times and bad times. In
my experience, the good times far outweigh the challenging times.
The good news is that you are empowered to make choices today
that will save you many years of heartache down the road. It is a
rewarding life.

Most importantly, you can do it. A joyful life is within your reach.
It is not a fairy tale and it is not reserved for a select few of God's
chosen ones to have. It is for all of us whom God has called to the
sacrament of marriage. You can find people who are miserable in
any walk of life. And this begs the question, is it the job or vocation,
or is it them?

I choose to be a joyful person. I don't always succeed, but I
choose daily to be happy and joyful in my marriage and in my relationships. It's not always easy, but it has been a freeing decision—

one that carries me into each passing day—one that gives me hope for even greater experiences in married life down the road.

I would leave you with this. I am a happily married man. This isn't by some stroke of luck or chance. Nor is it because I am a good boy who does what God instructs me to do. It is because I live the practical plan for marriage that God intended, that which is set forth in the preceding pages. In married life I didn't lose myself. I found myself, and now as a father I'm finding out even more of whom God created and has called me to be. I wouldn't trade places with anyone in the world.

This is just the beginning. These are the skills and tools needed for the first five years. And while some of them you will carry forward with you into the next five, ten, twenty, and more, each phase of marriage is different and will require you to grow, adapt, and change.

Chapter One: Crossing the Threshold and Unpacking Our Personal Baggage

1. Ronald Rolheiser, *Against an Infinite Horizon: The Finger of God in Our Everyday Lives* (New York: Crossroad, 2001), pp. 57–58.

2. United States Conference of Catholic Bishops (USCCB), *Follow the Way of Love: A Pastoral Message of the U.S. Catholic Bishops to Families on the Occasion of the United Nations 1994 International Year of the Family,* www.usccb.org/laity/follow.shtml.

3. Pope Benedict XVI, *Deus Caritas Est.* www.vatican.va/holy_ father/benedict/xvi/encyclicals/documents/hf_benxvi_enc_ 20051225_deus-caritas-est-en.html.

Chapter Two: Can You Hear Me Now? Communicating as Husband and Wife

1. For further reading and a more in depth discussion on the ways in which people express their love for one another I recommend reading Gary Chapman's *The Five Love Languages* (Chicago: Northfield, 1995).

Chapter Four: You Complete Me: Sex and the Christian Marriage

1. John and Stasi Eldredge, *Captivating: Unveiling the Mystery of a Woman's Soul* (Nashville: Thomas Nelson, 2007), pp. 131–132.

2. Daniel Homan, O.S.B. and Lonni Collins Pratt, *Radical Hospitality: Benedict's Way of Love* (Orleans, Mass.: Paraclete, 2002), pp. 140–142.

3. For further information please see Gary Smalley's DVD set *Hidden Keys to Loving Relationships* (Relationships Today, 1993).

Chapter Six: Married With Children—Openness to New Life

1. Pope Paul VI, *Gaudium et Spes,* Pastoral Constitution on the Church in the Modern World available on the Web at www.ewtn.com/library/Councils/v2modwor.htm, n. 50.

Chapter Seven: CSI: Marriage: Who's Right? Who's Wrong?

1. Sue Monk Kidd, *The Secret Life of Bees* (New York: Penguin, 2002), p. 92.

2. Mitch Albom, *Tuesdays with Morrie: An Old Man, a Young Man, and Life's Greatest Lesson* (New York: Doubleday, 1997), p. 149.

3. Rabbi Harold Kushner, *How Good Do We Have to Be?: A New Understanding of Guilt and Forgiveness* (Boston: Little, Brown, 1996), p. 113.

Chapter Nine: From Sole Survivor to Soul Survivors: Balancing An Individual and Couple Spirituality

1. Robert Wicks, *Living a Gentle, Passionate Life* (Mahwah, N.J.: Paulist, 1998), p. 49.

2. Wayne Muller, *Sabbath: Finding Rest, Renewal, and Delight in Our Busy Lives* (New York: Bantam, 2000), p. 8.

Albom, Mitch. *Tuesdays with Morrie: An Old Man, a Young Man, and Life's Greatest Lesson.* New York: Doubleday, 1997.

Pope Benedict XVI. *Deus Caritas Est.* www.vatican.va.

Chapman, Gary. *The Five Love Languages: How to Express Heartfelt Commitment to Your Mate.* Chicago: Northfield, 1995.

Eldredge, John and Stasi Eldredge. *Captivating: Unveiling the Mystery of a Woman's Soul.* Nashville: Thomas Nelson, 2007.

Homan, Daniel, O.S.B., and Lonni Collins Pratt. *Radical Hospitality: Benedict's Way of Love.* Orleans, Mass.: Paraclete, 2002.

Kidd, Sue Monk. *The Secret Life of Bees.* New York: Penguin, 2002.

Muller, Wayne. *Sabbath: Finding Rest, Renewal and Delight in Our Busy Lives,* New York: Bantam, 2000.

Kushner, Harold S. *How Good Do We Have to Be?: A New Understanding of Guilt and Forgiveness.* Boston: Little, Brown, 1996.

Pope Paul VI. "Pastoral Constitution on the Church in the Modern World," *Gaudium et Spes.* www.ewtn.com.

Rolheiser, Ronald. *Against an Infinite Horizon: The Finger of God in Our Everyday Lives.* New York: Crossroad, 2002.

United States Conference of Catholic Bishops (USCCB). *Follow the Way of Love: A Pastoral Message of the U.S. Catholic Bishops to Families on the Occasion of the United Nations 1994 International Year of the Family.* www.usccb.org.

Wicks, Robert. *Living a Gentle, Passionate Life.* Mahwah, N.J.: Paulist, 2000.

ABOUT THE AUTHOR

ROY PETITFILS is a professional school counselor and administrator at St. Cecilia Catholic School in Broussard, Louisiana. He is a counselor at Pax Renewal Center for Individual, Marriage, and Family Therapy. Author of *A Practical Guide to High School Campus Ministry*, he writes an internationally syndicated column, "Our Young Church." Roy, his wife, Mindi, and their sons, Maximillian and Benjamin, live in Youngsville, Louisiana, and are active members of Sacred Heart Church in Broussard. Roy served on the Diocesan Pastoral Council for his home diocese of Lafayette.